PRAISE FOR *THE ART OF UNEXPECTED SOLUTIONS*

Paul Sloane has hit another home run with this winner. If you only buy one business or self-improvement book this year it has to be this one. Paul brings his concepts to life with an amazing collection of examples of serendipitous successes. including a terrific history of many of the best and the worst business decisions in history. If you want to be a winner, get this book!
Brian McBride, former CEO of Amazon UK and President of the CBI

A great addition to the business bookshelf. It is packed with inspirational stories and practical tips to produce unexpected solutions.
Alistair Phelps, Senior Managing Director, Chief Strategy Officer, Nomura

A masterful guide to embracing creativity through curiosity and courage. *The Art of Unexpected Solutions* reminds us that true innovation is born from openness to surprise. This insightful, practical and inspiring read is a must for anyone looking to lead with imagination in an increasingly unpredictable world.
Tim Leney, MD, TCC Marketing Agency

The Art of Unexpected Solutions

Using lateral thinking to find breakthroughs

Paul Sloane

Publisher's note
Every possible effort has been made to ensure that the information contained in this book is accurate at the time of going to press, and the publishers and authors cannot accept responsibility for any errors or omissions, however caused. No responsibility for loss or damage occasioned to any person acting, or refraining from action, as a result of the material in this publication can be accepted by the editor, the publisher or the author.

First published in Great Britain and the United States in 2026

All rights reserved. No part of this publication may be reproduced, stored in a retrieval system or transmitted in any form or by any means – including electronic, mechanical, photocopying, recording or by any artificial intelligence (AI) or machine learning system – without the prior written permission of the publisher. Unauthorized use, including the use of text or images to train AI models, is strictly prohibited and may result in legal action.

Kogan Page
Kogan Page Ltd, 2nd Floor, 45 Gee Street, London EC1V 3RS, United Kingdom
Kogan Page Inc, 8 W 38th Street, Suite 902, New York, NY 10018, USA
www.koganpage.com

EU Representative (GPSR)
eucomply OÜ, Pärnu mnt 139b -14 11317, Tallinn, Estonia
www.eucompliancepartner.com

Kogan Page books are printed on paper from sustainable forests.

© Paul Sloane 2026

The moral rights of the author have been asserted in accordance with the Copyright, Designs and Patents Act 1988.

ISBNs

Hardback	9781398625952
Paperback	9781398625938
Ebook	9781398625945

Library of Congress Cataloging in Publication Data
A CIP record for this book is available from the Library of Congress.

British Library Cataloguing-in-Publication Data
A CIP record for this book is available from the British Library.

Typeset by Hong Kong FIVE Workshop, Hong Kong
Print production managed by Jellyfish
Printed and bound by CPI Group (UK) Ltd, Croydon CR0 4YY

*This book is dedicated to two unexpected
but joyous arrivals,
Dorothea and Bernadette*

CONTENTS

Introduction: A media upset 1

01 Why the unexpected is so important 5
Warfare 6
Politics 7
Science 8
Business 9
Sport 10
Summary 11

02 Spurn certainty and control 13
Summary 18

03 Welcome serendipity 19
The science of serendipity 23
Summary 25

04 Cultivate curiosity 27
Practical steps to develop your curiosity 30
Fostering organizational curiosity 32
Summary 33

05 Ask questions 35
The Google story: When audacious questions change the world 35

Contents

      The art of asking unexpected questions 38
      Ask a childlike question 40
      The neuroscience of questions 41
      Reclaim your questioning ability 42
      Create a question-rich environment 43
      Ask a question that no one else asks 44
      Questioning methods in problem analysis 45
      Make questions a daily practice 48

06 Challenge assumptions 51
      How can we challenge assumptions? 52
      Don Estridge and the IBM PC 54
      Assumptions and emotions 56
      Summary 57

07 Don't underestimate luck 59
      Make your own luck 64
      Summary 67

08 Build a culture of experimentation 69
      How can this be achieved in practice? 70
      Fostering processes for experimentation 72
      Changing the culture 73
      Summary 75

09 Ensure psychological safety 77
      Creating psychological safety in organizations 78
      Candour 79
      Overcoming a blame culture 81
      Summary 84

10 See what others miss 87
Observing customers 89
Positive deviants 91
Actions we can take to boost observation 93
Leadership and observation 94
Summary 95

11 Exploit mistakes 97
How do we achieve this in practice? 99
Summary 102

12 Turn obstacles into opportunities 105
How do we achieve this? 108
Summary 109

13 Unexpected actions in marketing 111
Examples 112
How to generate unexpected initiatives 115
Summary 116

14 Work in diverse fields 119
Polymaths 119
Intersections 122
Summary 124

15 Seize the unexpected opportunity 127
Tips at a corporate level 129
The minimum viable product 130
Viagra 131
Tips at a personal level 132
Summary 134

16 Why do we not seize opportunities? 137
Prejudices 137
Bias 140
Procrastination 141
Summary 144

17 Recognize hidden patterns 145
Cultivate pattern recognition skills 147
Alan Turing and the Enigma machine 148
Secondary consequences 149
Summary 150

18 Unexpected outcomes in the arts 153
Art 153
Literature 154
Music 156
Summary 157

19 Surprising combinations 159
Unexpected collaborations 162
Summary 163

20 Unexpected failures 165
The Titanic, 1912 165
The Maginot Line, 1940 166
Chernobyl, 1986 167
Segway personal transportation, 2001–2020 168
Friendster social network, 2002–2011 169
Amazon Fire phone, 2014–2015 169
Google Glass, 2014 170
Summary 171

21 Serendipitous collaborations 173
Examples 175
Fostering serendipitous connections 177
Summary 179

22 Put your product to another use 181
Examples 183
Summary 186

23 Trust your intuition 189
Recognizing intuition's limits 192
Summary 192

24 Play more 195
A recommended game 199
Summary 199

25 Welcome the random 201
Break the echo chamber 202
Practical ways to increase randomness 203
Overcoming resistance to randomness 205
The compound effect of embracing uncertainty 206
Summary 207

26 Tell more stories 209
Types of stories to tell 210
Summary 213

27 Accept productive boredom 215
The paradox of productive procrastination 216
The default mode advantage 217
Ways to find space for productive boredom 217
The art of marination 219
Summary 220

28 AI can aid the unexpected and innovation 223
Designing for serendipity 224
AI pattern recognition 225
Create the environment 226
AI risks 227
Recommendations for using AI 227
Summary 228

29 Build a physical environment for serendipity 231
Summary 235

Conclusion 237

Notes 239

Introduction

Along life's journey we encounter many unexpected outcomes, happy and sad. If you ask a number of your married friends how they met their partner, many will tell you that they met by chance. I certainly met my future wife through a lucky encounter. Similarly, I landed a good job following a chance meeting with an old university friend I had not seen for years. I am sure you have had many similar experiences. Serendipity is good luck in making fortunate and unexpected discoveries and much of this book concerns serendipity, but there are other sources of unexpected solutions and we will explore those too.

The most celebrated story of serendipity is that of Alexander Fleming, the Scottish scientist credited with the discovery of penicillin. In 1928, Fleming returned from a vacation to find a petri dish of bacteria cultures contaminated with mould. Frustrated by the contamination, he was about to discard the dish when he noticed something remarkable. The bacteria surrounding the mould had been destroyed. This accidental observation, a seemingly insignificant mishap, led to the development of penicillin and antibiotics, one of the most significant medical breakthroughs in history.

Fleming's discovery was not the result of meticulous planning or deliberate experimentation. It was born from a moment of unexpected disruption, a serendipitous encounter between bacteria and mould. But it also depended on Fleming's curiosity and determination to understand what was happening and then to develop the idea. This story serves as a powerful reminder that true innovation often arises from the unexpected, from the cracks in our carefully constructed plans.

Can you create conditions which favour serendipity and unexpected solutions? I believe that you can, and this book sets out to give you tips and advice on how to do that. These ideas and recommendations apply for individuals and groups. They apply in your personal life and at work – particularly if you lead a team.

We will explore how developing your curiosity, asking better questions and challenging assumptions can help you to generate more unexpected ideas and solutions. We will also show that at a corporate level it is essential to develop a culture of experimentation and psychological safety. You may be surprised to learn that the physical environment at work can foster or hinder collaboration and creativity.

One important precept is that serendipitous opportunities are of no use if they are not seized. We will look at why people miss out on opportunities and how not to. The aim of the book is to give you the tools and the inspiration to find more unexpected ideas and the encouragement to act on them.

Serendipity and luck are linked, but serendipity is more than luck. We can prepare for serendipity and create the conditions in which it can occur. This involves changing our mindset and the corporate culture. We need to change our attitude towards mistakes and failure. We can develop our curiosity. We can put in place processes for exploration and experimentation. We can develop our skills of observation and know where to look.

This book will look at each of these concepts in detail. It will explore the principles of serendipity in greater depth, providing practical strategies and real-world examples to help you harness the power of chance and unlock your creative potential. We will delve into the art of observation, the importance of divergent thinking and the role of intuition in navigating the unexpected.

I wish you good luck and fruitful unexpected outcomes.

01
Why the unexpected is so important

Think about the last time something genuinely surprised you. Maybe it was a shocking sports upset, a wild plot twist in a film that made you gasp, or maybe just bumping into an old friend in a city hundreds of miles from home. That feeling, the sudden jolt where the world doesn't quite work the way you thought it should, is a powerful and sometimes disturbing experience. The word 'unexpected' creates a potent image. It speaks of a deviation from the anticipated, a disruption of the familiar rhythms of life. But the unexpected is more than just a momentary surprise, it is a fundamental engine of change, a relentless shaper of our history and culture. From the battlefield to the laboratory, the political arena to the sports stadium, we see critical events shaped by the unexpected.

We spend most of our lives trying to plan, predict and control what happens next. But the truth is, the most important, game-changing moments in our lives are often the ones that come out of the blue. The unexpected isn't just an interruption to the story, it is the story. Life's most important moments are the ones we never see coming.

Fundamentally the unexpected is a direct challenge to our brains, which are basically prediction machines. Day in and day out, our minds build little models of reality, learning that if you do A, then B will happen. But when C happens instead, it throws a spanner in the works. This can be scary, such as in a 'black swan' event, a term coined by writer Nassim Nicholas Taleb for huge, shocking events like a global pandemic or a stock market crash that no one saw coming but which everyone tries to explain in hindsight as if they were obvious. But it can also be wonderful. That jolt of surprise is where creativity, learning and real change are born. It forces us to stop, look around and consider fresh possibilities.

Warfare

Nowhere is the power of the unexpected more starkly illustrated than in the field of warfare. Military history is a litany of battles won and lost not by the sheer weight of numbers or the superiority of arms, but by the audacious and the unforeseen. The Trojan Horse, a tale that has resonated for millennia, is the archetypal example of victory achieved through strategic deception, a fundamentally unexpected tactic. In more recent history, the German Blitzkrieg during World War II stunned the Allied forces. Fast-moving armoured divisions swept through neutral

Holland and Belgium and bypassed the massive defences of the Maginot Line. France fell within weeks. The success of the D-Day landings in Normandy hinged on a complex web of deception that convinced the Germans the main invasion would occur at the Pas-de-Calais, a masterful exploitation of the enemy's expectations. These events demonstrate a crucial military doctrine: surprise is a weapon, capable of paralyzing an adversary and creating windows of opportunity where none was thought to exist.

Politics

Politics is another arena in which the script is constantly being torn up. For decades, the Berlin Wall was the grim, concrete symbol of the Cold War. Its fall wasn't the result of a grand treaty but a moment of chaotic, unexpected confusion. In 1989, a mid-level East German official named Günter Schabowski was given a note about new, relaxed travel regulations to read at a press conference. He hadn't been properly briefed and when a journalist asked when the new rules would take effect, he mumbled, 'As far as I know... effective immediately, without delay.' The news spread like wildfire. Thousands of hopeful East Germans swarmed the checkpoints. The overwhelmed guards, with no clear orders, had no choice but to open the gates. A wall that had stood for 28 years fell because of a misunderstanding. It was a world-changing accident.

The election of Donald Trump in 2016 defied the predictions of nearly every major poll and political pundit, exposing deep-seated social and economic currents that had been largely invisible to the political establishment. Such unexpected moments of political rupture can lead to profound and lasting change.

Science

In the world of science, the unexpected is often the guest who gives. We think of scientists as methodical geniuses, but many of our biggest breakthroughs have come from pure, dumb luck combined with a curious mind. As mentioned earlier, the most famous example is Alexander Fleming, who returned from holiday in 1928 to find a petri dish with a mould which was resistant to bacteria. He had stumbled upon penicillin.

A similar thing happened with the discovery of the Big Bang's afterglow. In 1965, two astronomers, Arno Penzias and Robert Wilson, kept picking up a faint, annoying hiss on their radio antenna. They tried everything to get rid of it, even cleaning out pigeon droppings they thought might be the cause. It turned out that hiss wasn't bird poop, it was cosmic microwave background radiation, the leftover heat from the creation of the universe. They had accidentally stumbled upon the proof of the Big Bang.

In 1921, Frederick Banting and Charles Best were researching diabetes in dogs when they accidentally discovered insulin's crucial role. While trying to isolate pancreatic secretions, they found that extracts from the pancreas lowered blood sugar dramatically. This unexpected breakthrough transformed diabetes from a fatal disease into a manageable condition, saving millions of lives worldwide.

In November 1963, the crew of a fishing trawler off the coast of Iceland witnessed a shocking sight they mistook for a boat on fire. It was, in fact, something far more elemental: the birth of an island. A powerful, completely unexpected volcanic eruption had begun on the seabed, violently spewing ash and lava into the cold Atlantic. Within days, the accumulating material breached the surface, forming a new landmass. The eruption continued for more than three years, building an island that was named Surtsey, after the fire giant Surtr from Norse mythology. This surprising geological event provided a priceless opportunity. From its sterile, fiery birth, scientists have been able to meticulously document the arrival of life. Surtsey became a unique natural laboratory, offering a real-time window into how plants, insects and birds colonize a brand-new piece of earth, a process that continues to offer unexpected insights today.

Business

The business world is just as vulnerable to big surprises. For most of the 20th century, Kodak was photography. It sold the film, the paper and the cameras. It was a giant. Ironically, it even invented the first digital camera back in 1975. But the executives couldn't imagine a world without film, their main cash cow. They saw digital as a cute toy that would never have the quality of film. But it became a revolution. Kodak, the giant, went bankrupt.

Many business innovations and discoveries were the results of happy accidents. Viagra and Post-it Notes spring to mind. Both are mentioned in more detail later in the book.

Sport

Sport is all about rules and statistics, but the moments we remember forever are the ones that defy all expectations. The 'Miracle on Ice' at the 1980 Winter Olympics is a perfect example. A scrappy team of American college kids went up against the Soviet Union's professional ice hockey team, a legendary, invincible group that had dominated the sport for decades. It shouldn't have even been a contest. But somehow, the Americans won. It was more than a game, it was a moment of pure, unadulterated shock that gave a whole country a massive emotional lift. There was a similar shock when Leicester City won the English Premier League in 2016. At the start of the season, the odds of them winning were 5000 to 1. But week after week, this team of underdogs kept winning, right up until they lifted the trophy in one of the most astonishing upsets in sporting history. We love these stories because they prove that on any day, the impossible can happen.

Summary

While we continue to make our plans and fill our diaries, it's worth remembering that life's most profound and defining moments will likely be the ones we never anticipated. The unexpected is what keeps us on our toes. It's what fuels innovation, sparks revolutions and creates the legends we tell for generations. It's the universe's way of reminding us that the best parts of the story are the ones that haven't been written yet.

The unexpected is not a mere footnote to human progress, it is an integral and essential propulsive force. By disrupting our plans, challenging our assumptions and forcing us to adapt, unexpected events can be the catalysts for profound transformations.

How can we harness the power of the unforeseen? How can we prepare for or even encourage the unexpected? In this book I will try to show you how.

02
Spurn certainty and control

Before we can develop serendipity and encourage unexpected outcomes there are two passengers we need to throw overboard. We live in a world obsessed with the search for control and certainty. We believe that everything can and should be managed. From meticulously planned schedules to the relentless pursuit of perfection, we strive to exert control over every aspect of our lives. We carefully plan our days, our weeks, our years, attempting to navigate the unpredictable currents of existence with a firm hand on the tiller. But what if, instead of fighting against the tides of chance, we learned to harness their power? What if, instead of viewing uncertainty as an enemy, we embraced it as an opportunity for unexpected breakthroughs?

Creativity and innovation are unlikely to flourish in an environment of control. They thrive in the fertile ground of the unexpected, where chance encounters, unforeseen events and the unpredictable play a crucial role. The myth of control, the illusion that we can fully predict and manipulate the course of events, often hinders our ability to embrace the serendipitous moments that lead to the most profound discoveries.

Neuroscience reinforces this. While our brains are wired to crave certainty and react to unpredictability as a threat, it is in moments of quiet, not constant planning, that real insights appear. The default mode network in our brains, active when we're relaxed or daydreaming, is where creative connections form. We often overlook that some of our best ideas arrive when we're not consciously trying to control the outcome.

Across time and culture, there's been reverence for ambiguity. Taoist thinking invites us to flow with life's river rather than push against it. Zen Buddhism sees value in beginner's mind – the state of openness that precedes expertise. The great explorers of the Age of Discovery sailed into the unknown not with guarantees but with curiosity.

In the film *Conclave* (based on the book by Robert Harris), Cardinal Lawrence, played by Ralph Fiennes, leads the conclave to select a new pontiff after the Holy Father's death. He offers this profound meditation to his brother cardinals:

> My brothers and sisters, in the course of a long life in the service of our Mother the Church, let me tell you that the one sin I have come to fear more than any other is certainty. Certainty is the great enemy of unity. Certainty is the deadly enemy of tolerance. Even Christ was not certain at the end. '*Eli, Eli, lama sabachthani*?' he cried out in His agony at the ninth hour on the cross. 'My God, my God, why have you

forsaken me?' Our faith is a living thing precisely because it walks hand in hand with doubt. If there was only certainty, and if there was no doubt, there would be no mystery, and therefore no need for faith.

Mark Twain said, 'What gets us into trouble is not what we don't know. It's what we know for sure that just ain't so.' We are open-minded about what we don't know. We ask questions and listen. We ask no questions about the things of which we are sure. We are certain. We are in control. We are not open to unorthodox ideas, random input or unexpected events. Yet this is the area where great innovations often occur.

Adolphe Sax's invention of the saxophone is a classic example of uncertainty and chance in action. While attempting to improve the clarinet's tone and projection, Sax experimented with different shapes and materials. During this process, he accidentally created an instrument with a distinctive, powerful sound that was unlike anything else. Sax hadn't set out to invent something entirely new, but a fortunate combination of experimentation and unexpected results led to the birth of the saxophone. This chance discovery not only changed his career, it also transformed the world of music, introducing a completely new voice to orchestras and bands.

Harry Brearley was a researcher at Brown Firth Laboratories in Sheffield, England. In 1912 Brearley was asked by a weapons company to produce a metal which would not erode under fire as many small arms did. He alloyed steel with various fractions of chromium and carbon and tried to create an erosion-resistant steel. Instead, he stumbled upon stainless steel, which was highly resistant to corrosion. The story goes that he tossed one experimental result into the rubbish only to notice later that the steel had not rusted like all the other samples.

We can see from these examples that innovation results from the pursuit of experiment or the seizing of unexpected opportunity. It rarely involves the search for certainty. Indeed, the pursuit of control, while seemingly necessary, can often stifle creativity. When we focus solely on achieving pre-determined goals, we tend to narrow our focus, limiting our ability to see alternative paths and embrace new possibilities. We become so fixated on the intended outcome that we fail to recognize the value of detours, of unexpected twists and turns. We must acknowledge the limitations of our control, embrace the uncertainty of the journey and prepare ourselves for the unexpected. Only then can we truly begin to unlock the extraordinary potential that lies within the realm of chance.

In his book on cognitive biases, *Thinking, Fast and Slow*, Daniel Kahneman shows how our desire for certainty can lead to flawed decision-making.[1] One key concept is the certainty effect, where people irrationally favour guaranteed outcomes over probable ones, even when the latter offer better value. This bias can blind us to creative or unconventional solutions simply because they feel riskier or less familiar. Kahneman and his collaborator Amos Tversky showed that our brains often substitute difficult questions with easier ones, leading us to make quick, easy and wrong decisions.

Adam Grant builds on this in his book *Think Again*, arguing that overconfidence and cognitive rigidity prevent us from rethinking outdated beliefs.[2] He encourages 'confident humility', the ability to hold strong opinions loosely and revise them when new evidence emerges. Grant and Kahneman both emphasize that being wrong is not a failure but a step towards being less wrong. By acknowledging our blind spots and embracing doubt, we open ourselves to better alternatives and more innovative thinking. In a world that prizes decisiveness, their research reminds us that uncertainty is not weakness but wisdom in disguise.

Imagine an artist precisely planning every brushstroke, every colour, every line. While this approach may result in a technically proficient work, it may also stifle the spontaneity and intuition that are essential for true artistic expression. The most inspiring works of art often emerge from a process of experimentation, of allowing the creative impulse to flow freely, of embracing the unexpected.

The same principle applies to businesses and organizations. Rigid hierarchies, inflexible processes and a relentless focus on short-term gains can stifle innovation and hinder long-term growth. Companies that foster a culture of experimentation, that encourage their employees to take risks and embrace the unknown, are more likely to thrive in today's rapidly changing world.

Google famously adopted '20% Time', a policy that allowed employees to spend one fifth of their time on personal projects. This seemingly unconventional approach has led to the development of some of Google's most successful products, such as Gmail and Google Maps. By allowing employees the freedom to explore their own interests and pursue unexpected avenues, Google created an environment where serendipity can flourish.

Summary

Of course, embracing the power of chance does not mean abandoning all planning and structure. It means recognizing the limitations of our ability to predict the future and creating an environment that is receptive to the unexpected. It means cultivating a mindset of curiosity, of openness, of a willingness to explore the unknown.

This involves several key practices. First, we should cultivate a healthy level of curiosity. We need to ask questions, challenge assumptions and actively seek out new information and experiences. We have to change our attitude towards failure. It is important to see mistakes not as failures but as learning opportunities. We can then embrace the unexpected outcomes and explore the lessons they offer.

Instead of searching for complete certainty and control, we should welcome elements of doubt and ambiguity. That way we will be more receptive to strange and unexpected ideas and be able to pivot to exploit them. We need to disdain the effort to be certain in order to allow us to observe and exploit serendipity.

Questions

Do you like to be in control? To be certain of what is going on around you? How comfortable are you with uncertainty and doubt? What if some of the things you were certain about were wrong? Can you imagine that? How good are you at changing your mind? When did you last change your mind on an important issue?

03
Welcome serendipity

Serendipity is the occurrence of happy or beneficial discoveries by chance. It is a fortunate accident where you stumble upon something delightful or valuable without looking for it. Its wonder lies in its unpredictability. You have probably experienced it when finding a solution while looking for something else. You may have found some money in the pocket of a coat you have not worn for ages. Or you may have bumped into an old friend at the airport and found that you have much in common.

During World War II the British High Command wanted to attack the huge dams in the German Ruhr which supplied water and electricity to people and industry across a wide area. The dams were protected with torpedo nets so that torpedo bombs (which travel underwater) would be ineffective. While grappling with this problem the English engineer and inventor Barnes Wallis had a moment of serendipity. The story goes that he was watching his daughter skimming stones across the surface of a pond. This seemingly routine event sparked a brainwave from Wallis. His revolutionary idea was a bomb that could bounce over torpedo nets and into a dam's wall before sinking and detonating.

Wallis began experimenting in his garden, using his children's marbles to test the principle. The simple, serendipitous sight of a skimming stone, combined with Wallis's engineering genius, led to one of the most audacious and effective weapons of the war. Bouncing bombs were used by a bomber squadron known afterwards as the 'Dam Busters' to destroy the Möhne and Eder dams.

We can encourage serendipity in many ways. One is to foster collaboration with provocative thinkers, especially those operating in different fields from our own. Another is to create some space for play. In business we want more experimentation and exploration. At a more personal level we should allow time for unstructured play, chance and creative pursuits. Above all it is important to trust your instincts and learn to recognize the subtle signals that may point towards unexpected opportunities.

The creation of he Beatles track 'Revolution 9' perfectly captures the role of chance in artistic innovation. The track emerged almost accidentally as John Lennon, Yoko Ono and George Harrison experimented with tape loops and sound effects in the studio. They gathered a collection of random recordings, some made by the band, others found in the Abbey Road archives, and began splicing and looping them together without a clear plan. At one point, Lennon stumbled upon a test engineer's voice repeating the words 'Number nine', which became a central motif purely by chance. The process was chaotic, with tape machines running simultaneously and sounds being mixed live, leading to unexpected juxtapositions and even technical mishaps, like the tape running out and rewinding mid-track. What began as playful studio experimentation transformed, through a series of chance events and happy accidents, into one of the most avant-garde and controversial pieces in The Beatles' catalogue.

By embracing the power of chance, we can unlock our creative potential, navigate uncertainty with greater resilience and achieve breakthroughs that would be impossible to predict or plan. The journey may be erratic, but the rewards can be extraordinary.

Christian Busch defines three types of serendipitous discoveries.[3]

Archimedes Serendipity

This happens when a known problem is solved in an entirely unexpected way. The King of Syracuse asked the renowned thinker and mathematician Archimedes to verify that his new crown was made entirely of gold and not a mix of gold and silver. The story goes that Archimedes made a remarkable discovery while taking a bath. He saw how water overflowed when he entered the tub and realized that the volume of water displaced equalled the volume of any object totally submerged. This insight meant he could establish the exact volume and therefore the density of the crown. He did this and proved it was not pure gold. He had discovered the principle of buoyancy. Legend has it that he leapt out of the bath, exclaimed 'Eureka!' and ran naked into the street.

Fleming's discovery that led to penicillin would be another example of Archimedes Serendipity.

Post-it Note Serendipity

This occurs when a solution (or failed solution) to one problem leads to a solution for an altogether different problem. Spencer Silver was working as a researcher at 3M when he developed an unusual low-adhesive glue. It could stick lightly to surfaces and be removed without damage. However, he could see no practical application for it. Art Fry was a colleague of Silver's at 3M. He sang in a church choir and had a problem with paper bookmarks falling out of his hymnal. He realized that Silver's low-stick adhesive could solve this problem by creating bookmarks that stayed in place but could be repositioned when necessary. Fry and Silver developed the idea and Post-It Notes were launched by 3M in 1980. Their serendipitous collaboration transformed a failed adhesive into one of the world's most popular office supplies.

Adolphe Sax's accidental discovery of the saxophone would also represent Post-It Note Serendipity.

Thunderbolt Serendipity

This happens when no search or deliberate problem-solving is under way. A discovery is made in an entirely unexpected and surprising way – like a thunderbolt.

In the 1970s a technician called Scott Burnham, working for a music accessory company, connected the wires in a circuit incorrectly. The component made a weird moaning sound. Burnham adapted the strange wail into a guitar-pedal sound. He invented the Rat, a pedal that thousands of bands from Nirvana to Radiohead have used to enhance their music.

The science of serendipity

Serendipity is often perceived as a stroke of luck or chance, but it is in fact deeply rooted in the workings of the human brain and personality traits that shape how we perceive and respond to the world. Understanding the science behind serendipity reveals that it is not purely random but emerges from a complex interplay of cognitive processes, brain networks and psychological openness.

At the neurological level, one of the important factors in serendipitous insight is the brain's default mode network (DMN). The DMN is a collection of interconnected brain regions that become active when the mind is at rest, during daydreaming or quiet reflection. Far from being idle, the DMN is crucial for creative thinking and problem-solving. Recent brain-imaging studies have shown that the DMN initiates the generation of novel ideas by connecting the dots between random ideas and memories.[4] These initial creative sparks are then evaluated and refined by other brain networks responsible for control and attention. This dynamic collaboration explains why solutions or breakthroughs often occur unexpectedly, such as while taking a shower or going for a walk, moments when the brain is free to explore without focused effort.

But it is not just about brain wiring. Your personality has a lot to do with how often serendipity strikes. Psychologists talk about a trait called openness to experience, which plays a pivotal role in fostering serendipity. Openness is characterized by curiosity, imagination, intellectual flexibility and a willingness to explore new ideas and experiences.[5] Individuals high in openness tend to notice subtle patterns and connections that others might overlook, making them more receptive to unexpected opportunities. This trait also correlates with greater creativity, as open individuals are more likely to engage with diverse perspectives and synthesize novel solutions. Openness enhances mental flexibility, allowing people to adapt their thinking in uncertain or ambiguous situations, making conditions ripe for serendipitous discoveries.

There's also something to be said for being prepared and paying attention. Louis Pasteur said, 'Chance favours the prepared mind.' In other words, random events happen to everyone, but it's the curious, alert and open-minded who turn those accidents into something valuable. If you're always learning, exploring and reflecting on what you see, you're much more likely to catch those lucky breaks and make the most of them.

Another important ingredient is cognitive flexibility – basically, your brain's ability to switch gears and see things from different angles. People who are good at brainstorming and coming up with lots of ideas (what psychologists call 'divergent thinking') are more likely to stumble across unexpected solutions. When you combine this mental flexibility with the creative power of your brain's default mode, you're setting yourself up for those 'aha!' moments.

Importantly, the science of serendipity also highlights the role of mindfulness and presence. Being fully present and observant in everyday life increases the chances of noticing subtle cues and anomalies that otherwise might be ignored. Mindfulness sharpens awareness, allowing individuals to detect 'signals' in their environment that can trigger serendipitous connections.

Summary

I have experienced serendipity on many occasions, and I am sure that you have too. It is a strange phenomenon which involves fortune, attitude, preparedness, personality and mindset. It is not just luck but a product of how our brains generate creative ideas during moments of rest, how our openness to new experiences shapes our perception, and how our preparedness and attentiveness enable us to recognize and act on unexpected opportunities. By understanding these scientific underpinnings, we can better cultivate the conditions, both internal and external, that invite serendipity into our lives.

> **Questions**
>
> Take a moment to list any examples of serendipity in your life or career. When did you benefit from a piece of pure luck? When did you seize a chance opportunity? What were the circumstances?
>
> What lessons can you learn from these experiences?

04
Cultivate curiosity

Legend has it that when he was a boy, the great inventor, astronomer and scientist Galileo Galilei was sitting in church when he became curious about the swinging chandelier which held incense. Using his own pulse to measure timing he determined that the swings were regular. He deduced that the period of a pendulum was constant and not dependent on the weight of the pendulum or the initial displacement; it was dependent only on the length of the rope. His curiosity sparked his lifelong study of pendulums and gravity.

Galileo's discoveries extended into many fields. He was fascinated by a recent Dutch invention – the telescope. Galileo was the first to use a telescope for systematic scientific and astronomical observations. In 1609, he improved upon the Dutch design and was the first to point a telescope at the night sky, leading to groundbreaking discoveries such as the moons of Jupiter, the phases of Venus and the mountains on the Moon. His work laid the foundations for modern physics and astronomy, challenging old beliefs and advancing science profoundly.

There is an old proverb, 'Curiosity killed the cat', but this is bad advice. Curiosity is the fuel of creativity, discovery and innovation. As we go through our formal education, a subtle but insidious shift occurs. The open-ended questions that once sprang from our lips are gradually replaced by a demand for definitive answers. We're rewarded for knowing, not for asking. The systematic suppression of curiosity stifles individual potential but also cripples creativity. The relentless pursuit of 'knowing' can be the enemy of discovery.

Many of you will have experienced how, in the corporate world, curiosity is discouraged. The emphasis is on efficiency and productivity rather than questioning and experimentation. The prevailing mantra is 'stick to what you know' rather than 'explore what you don't'. We are encouraged to specialize, to master a specific skill set and to remain within the comfortable confines of our expertise. But often the most interesting ideas and the most fruitful innovations lie at the intersection of seemingly disparate disciplines.

George de Mestral, a Swiss engineer, was walking his dog in the Alps when he noticed burrs clinging stubbornly to his clothing and to his dog's fur. Instead of simply brushing them off and dismissing them as a nuisance, de Mestral's curiosity was piqued. He examined the burrs under a microscope and observed their tiny hooks, which allowed them to latch onto fabric. This simple act of curiosity led to the invention of Velcro, a revolutionary fastening system that has transformed industries ranging from clothing to aerospace.

Many people would have dismissed the burrs as an annoyance. What if de Mestral had lacked the curiosity to investigate their unique structure? The world would have been deprived of an innovative solution, a solution that emerged not from specialized knowledge or rigorous planning but from a simple act of curiosity and observation. Innovative thinkers are fascinated by unexpected events which arouse their curiosity, not their annoyance.

Curiosity is not merely a desirable trait; it is the lifeblood of innovation. It is the engine that drives us to ask, 'What if?' and 'Why not?' It is the spark that ignites our imagination and compels us to explore uncharted territories. Curiosity can be a major driver of innovation, yet too often we allow it to be extinguished by the pressures of conformity and the fear of failure.

In 1943 naval engineer Richard James was working on the problem of how to stabilize sensitive ship equipment at sea. He was using coiled springs and accidentally knocked one off of a shelf. He was fascinated to see that it seemed to walk down and come to rest in a standing position. He was curious as to what purpose this property might be put. James's wife Betty said, 'He came home and said, "I think if I got the right property of steel and the right tension, I could make it walk."'

James carried out many experiments with different types of steel wire and finally, after a year of trials, he found a spring that would 'walk'. He had invented the 'Slinky'. He saw the possibilities for it as a toy when children in the neighbourhood were excited by it. The first order of Slinkys arrived at Gimbels department store in Philadelphia in November 1945 and sold out in 90 minutes.

Practical steps to develop your curiosity

Curiosity is like a muscle: the more you use it, the stronger it gets. Cultivating curiosity is not about magically acquiring knowledge but about deliberately adopting a mindset that questions, explores and embraces the unknown. It's about rekindling the childlike wonder that allows us to see the world with fresh eyes, transforming passive observation into active inquiry.

First, we must actively challenge our assumptions. Our assumptions can act as mental barriers, preventing us from seeing new possibilities. We must constantly question our beliefs, even those that seem self-evident. What are we taking for granted? What are we overlooking? What are the hidden assumptions that are shaping our perception of the problem? Consider again George de Mestral and his discovery that led to Velcro. What were the ingrained assumptions he could have made? He might have simply assumed burrs were a nuisance, a mundane aspect of nature to be brushed away. Instead, his curiosity led him to challenge these assumptions. He didn't assume their stickiness was accidental or unimportant; he questioned how and why they adhered so effectively. This act of questioning the 'obvious' is precisely what challenging assumptions entails, leading to groundbreaking solutions that others overlook.

Second, we must embrace experimentation. Innovation is rarely a linear process; it is often a messy, iterative journey of trial and error. We must be willing to experiment, to take risks and to accept that failure is an inevitable part of the learning process. As Thomas Edison supposedly said, 'I have not failed. I've just found 10,000 ways that won't work.' Edison viewed failure not as a setback but as an opportunity to learn and refine his approach. By embracing experimentation, we create a safe space for curiosity to flourish.

Third, we must foster a culture of intellectual humility. This means acknowledging the limits of our knowledge and being open to learning from others, regardless of their background or expertise. It means recognizing that we don't have all the answers and that there is always more to discover. It also means that we must be willing to admit when we are wrong and to change our minds in the face of new evidence.

Fourth, we must look in places we normally don't visit. We must speak to people we normally don't encounter. We should read articles and books in fields we normally ignore. We should deliberately step into the unknown – just out of pure curiosity.

Consider the concept of 'cross-pollination', the process of drawing inspiration from seemingly unrelated fields. Some of the most groundbreaking innovations have emerged from the unexpected connections between disparate disciplines. For example, the field of biomimicry draws inspiration from nature to solve complex engineering problems. By studying the intricate designs of natural systems, engineers have developed innovative solutions for everything from energy efficiency to materials science.

Fostering organizational curiosity

While individual curiosity is vital, the corporate world often inadvertently stifles it. To truly unleash innovation, organizations must actively cultivate a curious environment. This requires a shift from strict adherence to established norms to embracing exploration and questioning. Companies can implement several initiatives to foster this change.

One effective approach is to dedicate specific time for 'Curiosity Hours' or 'Innovation Sprints'. These are designated periods during which employees are encouraged to explore novel ideas, research unrelated topics or work on passion projects without immediate performance pressures. This provides the mental space necessary for divergent thinking. Furthermore, promoting cross-functional collaboration programmes can be highly beneficial. By encouraging teams from different departments to work together on seemingly unrelated problems, organizations can foster organic cross-pollination of ideas, leading to unexpected insights.

Another powerful tool is 'reverse mentoring', where junior employees or individuals from diverse backgrounds are empowered to share their perspectives and questions with senior leaders. This approach challenges ingrained assumptions and encourages a fresh look at long-standing practices. Similarly, creating failure forums or lessons-learned sessions provides a safe space for teams to openly discuss experiments that didn't yield desired results, emphasizing learning and adaptation over blame. Finally, leaders themselves must actively role model curiosity. By visibly asking open-ended questions, admitting when they don't know something and actively seeking diverse opinions, they create a culture where questioning is not just tolerated but celebrated.

Ultimately, encouraging curiosity is not simply about acquiring more knowledge, it is about cultivating a mindset, a way of approaching the world with a sense of wonder and a relentless desire to learn. It is about embracing uncertainty, challenging assumptions and fostering a culture of intellectual humility.

Summary

By rekindling our curiosity, we can unlock a world of unexpected solutions and fuel the innovations that will shape our future. Don't let 'certainty' blind you – embrace the questions, embrace the unknown and embrace the transformative power of curiosity. If you want to find unexpected solutions, don't become complacent and just accept what you see. Keep asking 'Why?' and 'What if?' and you will be on your way to cultivating breakthrough ideas. The status quo and conventional thinking are rarely the route to innovation and progress.

> ### Questions
>
> Think of a big challenge at work or in your personal life. What questions would a curious child ask about this issue? Write down several. What questions would a super-intelligent alien ask? What would the Spanish artists Picasso or Dalí or the Dalai Lama ask about this issue? Force yourself to be much more curious about the situation and the assumptions you are making.

05
Ask questions

Questions are the tools we use to explore and understand our world. Children learn by asking questions. Students and apprentices learn by asking questions. But many adults ask few questions. They think they know most of what they need to know. Curious people ask many questions. They are open-minded and receptive to new ideas. Let's look at the power of asking questions. We will consider different types of question and review some questioning methods.

The Google story: When audacious questions change the world

Lawrence Page was born in 1973 to Carl and Gloria Page, who both worked at Michigan State University. Larry took up programming at the age of six. He went on to study business and computer science at his parents' university before applying to MIT. He was rejected and eventually went to Stanford, which proved a happy choice. In his first year he met second-year graduate student

Sergey Brin. The two hit it off and became friends. They were both smart, rebellious and geeky. They argued a lot. Page later said, 'I thought Sergey was pretty obnoxious. He had really strong opinions about things and I guess I did, too.'

Brin was born in Moscow in 1974 to Jewish parents. Both his parents were mathematicians but their prospects in Russia were limited. In 1979 they emigrated to the USA. Like Larry Page, the young Sergey received a Commodore 64 as a present and programmed it. He graduated from the University of Maryland with a degree in mathematics and computer science.

Both young men were both fascinated by the World Wide Web, which was exploding in use in the mid-1990s. Page wrote his dissertation on how to assess the relative importance of different web pages. He was inspired by the academic research practices of his parents. He knew that one way to judge the importance of a research paper was to count how many other research papers reference it as a source. Page wanted to do something similar with web pages, but although it was easy to see how many links went out from a page, it was difficult to see how many other sites linked to it. Then he asked an audacious question: 'What if we could download the whole of the World Wide Web and analyse all its links?'

At that time, in early 1996, there were more than 100,000 websites, with over 10 million documents and around 1 billion links. And the numbers were growing exponentially. Page, however, was undaunted. After persistent requests, his supervisor eventually allowed him to download the entirety of the web onto the university server. He then built a crawler, which was designed to go through the whole web, site by site, and check stored links and addresses. The project was called Backrub and it quickly grew to huge proportions. It absorbed over half of Stanford's entire web bandwidth and caused the university server to crash. Thankfully for Page, the university authorities recognized the potential of his creation and allowed him to continue. He also impressed his friend Brin, who quickly joined the project.

At this point, they were still building a web analysis tool. Page later said, 'Amazingly, I had no thought of building a search engine. The idea wasn't even on the radar.' As their project developed, they came up with smarter ways to assess the value of a page based on the number and quality of incoming links. They then realized that they had discovered the basis for a search engine that would be more valuable than anything currently available. They honed their approach so that they not only counted the number of incoming links but assigned a higher value to a link coming from a site with many incoming links. This method distinguished their technology and assessed the relative importance of sites with greater accuracy than competing models.

Page and Brin called their search engine Google. They wanted to use the word Googol, which is the number 1 followed by 100 zeros. But Googol.com was already taken, so they settled for Google.com. In April 1998 they published a paper explaining their approach without giving away the exact details.

In order to commercialize the project, they approached the CEOs of the leading search companies of the day

– Yahoo!, Alta Vista, Lycos and Excite. They presented their case and asked for $1 million to license their patents and tools. In each case they were turned down. Page said later, 'It was not a significant expense to them. But it was a lack of insight at the leadership level. A lot of them told us, "Search is not that important."' How did the big players get it so wrong? They believed that the key to gaining traffic and advertising was to add more content. They thought that people would explore the web rather than search the web.

Page and Brin founded Google in 1998. It went on to wipe out all the big players who had turned down the two students.

There are three important lessons here. First, the power of an audacious question, 'What if we could download the whole of the World Wide Web and analyse all its links?' A question that few people would have even contemplated. Second, the power of allowing bright people to run experiments with little control or supervision. Third, that in looking for one thing, the ranking of pages, they discovered something else – a powerful search tool.

The art of asking unexpected questions

The most transformative breakthroughs often come from questions that seem to defy conventional wisdom. While most people ask predictable questions within established frameworks, innovators learn to ask questions that others wouldn't even think to consider. These unexpected questions can shatter assumptions, reveal hidden opportunities and open entirely new pathways to solutions.

Consider the story of Reed Hastings, the co-founder, with Marc Randolph, of Netflix. In 1997, after being charged a $40 late fee for a VHS video rental, most people would have asked, 'How can I avoid late fees in the future?' But Hastings asked an unexpected question: 'What if there were no late fees at all?' This simple but radical question led to the creation of a subscription model that revolutionized the entertainment industry. He didn't stop there – later, when the company was successful with DVD-by-mail, he asked another unexpected question: 'What if we competed with ourselves?' This led to the development of streaming services that eventually made their own DVD business obsolete.

The key to asking unexpected questions lies in challenging the fundamental assumptions that everyone else takes for granted. In the medical field, Dr Barry Marshall asked an unexpected question about stomach ulcers. While the medical establishment firmly believed ulcers were caused by stress and spicy food, Marshall asked, 'What if ulcers are actually caused by bacteria?' This question was so radical that he had to infect himself with the bacteria to prove his theory. His unexpected question led to a Nobel Prize and transformed treatment for millions of patients.

To develop your ability to ask unexpected questions, practise the following techniques:

- First, identify the core assumptions everyone makes about your challenge. Then systematically question each assumption by asking, 'What if the opposite were true?'
- Second, borrow perspectives from completely unrelated fields. A biologist might ask how nature solves similar problems, while an artist might focus on aesthetic or emotional dimensions.
- Third, imagine you're from another planet or time period – what questions would you ask about our current approaches that we never consider?

The most powerful unexpected questions often sound naive or even foolish at first. But as Reed Hastings, Barry Marshall and countless other innovators have proven, these seemingly simple questions can unlock extraordinary possibilities that conventional thinking would never discover.

Ask a childlike question

Children learn by asking questions. Little children ask hundreds of questions a day. Many of these are remarkable and challenge our assumptions and view of the world.

Edwin Land was an American inventor who had studied chemistry. On holiday in 1943, he took a photograph of his three-year-old daughter. She asked why she could not see the result straight away and she kept asking. Land pondered this question and an idea formed in his mind.

He went on to develop the Polaroid camera, a revolutionary product which sold over 150 million units and made Land into a celebrity. His daughter's naive question had led him to challenge the assumptions that the whole photography industry took for granted.

The neuroscience of questions

Recent research in neuroscience reveals why children are such natural questioners and why this ability often diminishes with age. When we ask questions, our brains release dopamine, the same neurotransmitter associated with pleasure and reward. This creates a positive feedback loop that makes questioning inherently satisfying. Children's brains are particularly primed for this questioning behaviour because they are in a critical learning phase where curiosity is essential for survival and development.

However, as we age, social conditioning often discourages questioning. We learn to conform, to avoid appearing ignorant and to accept established ways of doing things. The educational system, while well-intentioned, often rewards having the 'right' answers rather than asking interesting questions. This gradually erodes our natural curiosity and questioning instincts.

Reclaim your questioning ability

The good news is that we can reactivate our questioning abilities. Studies show that adults who practise regular questioning exercises can significantly improve their creative problem-solving skills. One effective technique is the 'five-year-old exercise' – before tackling any problem, spend five minutes asking the kinds of questions a curious child would ask, even if they seem obvious or silly.

Another powerful approach is to regularly spend time with children. Their unfiltered questions often reveal blind spots in our thinking. Many successful entrepreneurs and inventors make it a point to explain their ideas to children, not just to simplify their thinking but to capture the fresh perspectives that childlike curiosity provides.

If it is obvious that asking questions is such a powerful tool, why do we stop asking them? For some people it comes down to laziness. Others are in such a hurry to get on with things that they do not stop to ask questions because it might slow them down. They risk rushing headlong into the wrong actions. They assume they know all the main things they need to know and they do not bother to ask more. They cling to their beliefs and remain certain in their assumptions. Other people are afraid that by asking questions they will look weak, ignorant or unsure. They like to give the impression that they are decisive and in command of the relevant issues. They fear that asking questions might introduce uncertainty or show them in a poor light.

In fact, asking questions is a sign of strength and intelligence – not a sign of weakness or uncertainty. Great leaders constantly ask questions and are well aware that they do not have all the answers.

Create a question-rich environment

Organizations that thrive on innovation understand the importance of creating cultures in which questioning is not just accepted but actively encouraged. Google's famous '20% time' policy, where employees can spend one-fifth of their time on personal projects, is fundamentally about creating space for questioning and exploration. Similarly, Amazon's 'Day 1' mentality encourages employees to maintain a startup-like curiosity regardless of the company's size.

To foster better questioning in your own environment, consider implementing 'question quotas' – meetings where participants must ask at least three questions before offering solutions. Create 'assumption audits' where teams systematically question the fundamental beliefs underlying their strategies. Most importantly, reward and celebrate good questions, not just good answers.

Ask a question that no one else asks

Every year millions of babies around the world die within the first week of birth. Many could be saved with the use of incubators, which are widely available in the developed world but not in underdeveloped countries. Much of the medical equipment that is donated to hospitals in these countries falls into disuse because of the lack of spare parts or shortage of trained technicians.

The conventional approach to this kind of problem would be to design a low-cost robust incubator with some redundancy and some spare parts. However, Tim Prestero, CEO at a company called Design That Matters, took a more lateral approach. Instead of asking the conventional question 'How can we build a low-cost incubator that does not break down?', he asked, 'What equipment, if any, is easily maintained in the developing world?' The answer to that question was cars – more specifically, Toyota cars. Most towns have garages with mechanics who can service and repair Toyotas. So Prestero's company designed an incubator made out of car parts.

'Some incubator parts – where the baby lies, casters in the front for braking and steering, and a chrome handrail for carrying – are standard issue,' said Prestero. 'But after that, the automobile parts come in. The incubator prototype functions using electricity, but it has a motorcycle battery as a backup in case the lights go out. Headlights generate heat and an HVAC (heating, ventilation and air-conditioning) fan blows it around. An engine-intake filter removes dust, bugs and pathogens. Turn signals function as visual alarms if the baby is in trouble.'

Ask more questions and you will get more answers. Ask unexpected questions and you will get unexpected answers.

Questioning methods in problem analysis

I run workshops on lateral thinking and innovation. We might start the day with some big questions, such as:

- How can we recruit and retain excellent staff?
- How can we change our culture to be more adventurous and less risk averse?
- How can we become more innovative?

We do not immediately start coming up with ideas. Instead, I ask participants to analyse the problem by asking why and then why again and again. So we reframe the challenge into something like:

- Why is it difficult to recruit top staff?
- Why are we risk averse?
- Why are we not innovative?

For each answer, we ask why again. This approach is based on the '5 Whys' technique developed by Toyota, under Sakichi Toyoda, in the 1930s. This iterative questioning method involves asking 'why' repeatedly. It seeks to drill down past symptoms to the true underlying cause of an issue. This became the basis of the management technique known as root cause analysis, which uses this questioning approach to enable effective and lasting solutions rather than simply temporary fixes.

Another questioning method I use in my workshops involves 'What if' scenarios. This technique encourages breakthrough thinking by temporarily suspending constraints and exploring possibilities. Walt Disney famously used this approach when developing Disneyland, asking, 'What if we could create a place where adults and children could have fun together?' This question led to innovations that transformed the entertainment industry.

'What if' questions work because they bypass our logical filters and allow us to explore possibilities that our rational minds might immediately dismiss. They are particularly effective when facing seemingly impossible challenges or when existing solutions have reached their limits. The key is to ask 'What if' questions that challenge core assumptions about resources, timeframes, technologies or market conditions.

Another powerful framework is 'Constraint Questioning' where you systematically identify and question each constraint you believe limits your options. Often, constraints that seem immutable are actually assumptions that can be challenged or worked around with creative approaches.

A further questioning method I often use is 'Six Serving Men'. It is used as a team exercise that examines an issue from 12 different viewpoints. It is based on the words of the poem by Rudyard Kipling:

> I keep six honest serving men
>   (They taught me all I knew);
> Their names are What and Why and When
>   And How and Where and Who.

We probe the topic using these questioning words from both a positive and a negative perspective. The issue is defined as a question and then 12 sheets of flipchart paper are arranged around the room. On each sheet, one of the 12 questions is written as the heading and the team then comes up with answers to that question. Suppose the issue is, 'How can we improve customer service in our retail centres?' The questions could be constructed as follows:

1. What is good customer service?
2. What is bad customer service?
3. Why do we get good customer service?
4. Why do we get bad customer service?
5. When is there good customer service?
6. When is there bad customer service?
7. How do we get good customer service?
8. How do we get bad customer service?
9. Where is there good customer service?
10. Where is there bad customer service?
11. Who gives good customer service?
12. Who gives poor customer service?

By repeatedly approaching the questions of good service and bad service and by forcing people to come up with new answers and inputs, a broad picture is painted of the issue and the underlying factors. The ideas on the sheets are analysed, prioritized and combined to give a deeper understanding of the problem and some insights as to why it is happening. These ideas then become the starting point for a plan to address the issue.

Make questions a daily practice

The most successful questioners don't just ask questions during formal problem-solving sessions – they make questioning a daily habit. This means developing what psychologists call 'question sensitivity' – the ability to notice when questions need to be asked. Start each day by asking yourself three questions about your priorities, assumptions and opportunities. End each day by questioning what you learned, what surprised you and what you might do differently.

Professional development should include regular 'question training', just as we practise other skills. This might involve keeping a question journal, practising different questioning techniques, or joining groups focused on inquiry and exploration. The investment in developing your questioning abilities pays dividends in every area of life, from personal relationships to professional challenges.

Remember that great questions often lead to more questions rather than immediate answers. Embrace this process of expanding inquiry rather than rushing to closure. The most profound insights often emerge not from the first question you ask but from the questions that your initial questions inspire.

> **Questions**
>
> Think of a challenge in your work or personal life. Write down 10 obvious questions to ask about the challenge. Now write 10 childlike, audacious or unexpected questions. Go through the list slowly and see if any of the questions stimulate remarkable, fresh and useful ideas. This exercise works well on your own but even better in a small, diverse group.

06
Challenge assumptions

Every time that we approach a problem, in any walk of life, we bring to bear assumptions that limit our ability to conceive fresh solutions. Our experiences condition us to see any new situation in terms of situations we have seen before. Assumptions are mental shortcuts. They allow us to make decisions quickly without having to check everything first. For example, when I get into a taxi I assume that the driver is competent and knows the area. Our assumptions are based on past experiences and they are usually right. But in business, when faced with an unusual or complex situation, our assumptions can create dangerous barriers to fresh ideas. We make assumptions unconsciously and put things into a framework with constraints that limit our thinking. Innovative thinkers are always aware of assumptions and deliberately confront them.

We often don't realize that we are making assumptions because they feel natural. But when we take them for granted, we limit our ability to see alternative perspectives, solutions or dangers.

Bernie Madoff orchestrated one of history's largest Ponzi schemes, defrauding investors out of billions of dollars. His deception thrived because people assumed that he was reputable and trustworthy. He was a respected Wall Street figure, who had served as chairman of Nasdaq. He promised consistently high returns, which many assumed were plausible given his reputation. Private investors, corporations, banks and charities failed to scrutinize his operations. He used money from new investors to repay earlier ones. When the scheme collapsed in 2008, thousands lost their life savings. Bernie Madoff's Ponzi scheme is estimated to have defrauded investors out of over $60 billion. He was sentenced to 150 years and he died in prison in 2021.

Challenging assumptions can protect us from dangers, but it is also a critical strategy that has led to many clever solutions and groundbreaking discoveries. In 1900 many believed that human flight was impossible. The prevailing assumption was that heavier-than-air machines could not fly. The Wright brothers challenged this assumption. They focused on experimentation. By defying conventional beliefs they achieved the first powered flight in 1903, changing the course of history.

How can we challenge assumptions?

Innovators know that assumptions are there to be challenged and they relish defying them. How can you do this? Here are some tips.

Start by recognizing that you and everyone else have ingrained assumptions about every situation. Challenging assumptions doesn't mean rejecting everything. It means being aware of the beliefs that underpin your thinking and testing whether they really hold true.

Ask many basic questions in order to discover and challenge assumptions. Use the methods outlined in the previous chapter. Ask 'What if?' questions. For example, What if this was wrong? What if we were starting from scratch with no constraints? What if we had an unlimited budget? What if we had no budget? Or use the '5 Whys' method, popularized by Toyota. Ask why and for each answer ask why again. Do this five times to get to the root cause of the problem. Often, this method will uncover assumptions and hidden beliefs that can be challenged.

Another good question to ask is, 'What if the opposite were true?' No taxi company questioned the assumption that taxi companies need taxis. But Travis Kalanick did when he founded Uber in San Francisco in 2009. What are the basic beliefs that underpin your business model? For each, consider more than something different – start by considering the opposite.

Write a list of all the ground rules and assumptions that apply in your environment and then go through the list and ask, 'What would happen if we deliberately broke this rule?' 'What if we did the opposite of the norm?'

Pretend you are a complete outsider and ask questions like 'Why do we do it this way at all?'. Or better still, bring in an outsider. People from completely different fields often see things you don't. They are not bound by the same assumptions. Invite them to review your situation. Their questions can reveal blind spots.

Don Estridge and the IBM PC

Don Estridge, 'the father of the IBM PC', was the man who challenged every assumption in the IBM rule book in order to ship a revolutionary product, the IBM personal computer, which spawned a whole industry and ushered in a new era in the history of computing. Estridge was born in 1937 in Jacksonville, Florida. He gained a bachelor's degree in electrical engineering from the University of Florida. He worked for the army and then joined IBM, working in the 1960s at NASA's Goddard Space Flight Center.

The 1970s saw IBM dominate the mainframe computer arena, but smaller companies were springing up fast with mini-computers and home computers. IBM promoted Estridge to lead the team that developed its first mini-computer, the Series /1. It was not a great success and he was assigned a staff position. However, in 1980 he took charge of the IBM entry-level systems and was given the objective of developing an inexpensive personal computer to take on the upstarts like Atari, Apple and Commodore.

Estridge realized that he could not create a viable competitive product and bring it to market quickly if he used standard IBM development processes. At that time IBM maintained total control of all its manufacturing with proprietary designs from power supplies to integrated circuits to operating systems. Estridge decided to bypass this heavy-duty approach and instead to go outside the company for third-party components and software. Even more radically, Estridge opted for an 'open architecture'.

He published the specifications of the IBM PC, thus enabling a burgeoning industry of suppliers of add-ons, hardware and software products. The product included expansion card slots specifically to take external offerings.

'When we started,' Estridge said, 'we were a dozen people who knew a little about personal computers.' The engineers in his small team had all come from the world of large computers and the biggest task was to get them to think completely differently about computers. 'The most important thing we learned was that how people reacted to a personal computer emotionally was almost more important than what they did with it,' he recalled. 'That was an entirely new lesson in computer design.'

In four months Estridge and his team developed a prototype and within one year the IBM PC was on retail shelves, a record time for product development in the giant company. The product was launched in August 1981. Competitors were initially unworried because they were shipping higher-specification machines of their own design, but the open architecture proved a key competitive advantage and the IBM product quickly came to dominate the market. Its success led to the formation of companies like Compaq and Dell, which specialized in 'PC clone' products.

Estridge was promoted several times at IBM and in 1984 became Vice President, Manufacturing. He turned down a lucrative offer from Steve Jobs to become President of Apple Computers.

Not all his products were successful, however. His team developed the PCjr home computer, which flopped.

However, he was sanguine about it. 'You have to take risks in this business,' he said, 'or it's no fun.'

In 1985 Estridge and his wife Mary Ann were killed when the plane they were travelling in crashed at Dallas. Estridge was 48 years old. At the time of his death the IBM PC group had grown to 10,000 employees and was grossing about $4.5 billion a year. If it had been a separate entity, it would have been the third largest computer company in the world behind IBM and DEC.

Assumptions and emotions

Beliefs are often deeply held. Challenging cherished assumptions is not just an intellectual exercise, it can be emotional too. People can feel uncomfortable or even threatened by the process. We often link our corporate identity to our core beliefs. When we acknowledge that an assumption was wrong, we are admitting we were wrong. The process needs to be handled carefully. It is important to stress that growth comes from change and change can be uncomfortable. The most successful innovators, leaders and thinkers are those who are willing to admit they were wrong and have the courage to change their minds. It is better to be right in the long run.

Psychologists have long studied how our brains love to cling to assumptions. One culprit is confirmation bias, our tendency to seek out information that supports what we already believe and ignore evidence that challenges it. Another is the status quo bias, a preference for things to stay the same. Both of these mental shortcuts keep us in our comfort zones but blind us to potentially better paths.

That's why great innovators develop tools to expose these blind spots. Jeff Bezos popularized the idea of 'disagree and commit' at Amazon. He encourages leaders to voice doubts and test deeply held beliefs rather than accept consensus.

To cultivate this mindset, try conducting a simple 'Assumption Audit'. Pick a process, belief or product. Write down everything that's taken for granted. Then challenge each point: *What if this weren't true? What if we started from scratch?* Or ask, *What if we've been looking at this the wrong way all along?* Try solving the problem under absurd constraints. Often, bold ideas emerge when we remove the obvious.

Summary

Challenging assumptions is not about being contrarian for the sake of it – though that can be a fun part of the process. It is about being curious and open to new possibilities. It means being prepared to explore the unknown. We have to recognize that the world is constantly changing, and what was true yesterday may not be true tomorrow.

In business we have to become rule breakers. Don Estridge broke every rule in the IBM book. He was forgiven. The larger an organization becomes, the more rules, assumptions and conventions it has. Leaders need to create an environment where breaking rules is allowed and even encouraged. For many years Hewlett Packard awarded a so-called Medal of Defiance to someone who had broken conventions in order to solve a problem or benefit a customer.

The art of finding unexpected solutions begins with the courage to ask, 'What if we are making some wrong assumptions here?' Questions like that have the power to unlock new ideas, new paths and new possibilities.

Ken Olsen was CEO of DEC (Digital Equipment Corporation), a company that was a great innovator in the days of the mini-computer. Olsen said, 'The best assumption to have is that any commonly held belief is wrong.'

Questions

Think of an organization that you know well. List five or six beliefs that are strongly held by the executives of that organization. Now challenge each of these assumptions. Ask: What if the opposite were true?

07
Don't underestimate luck

We underestimate the power and importance of luck. We attribute positive outcomes to good management and skill. We attribute bad outcomes to poor management and incompetence. But very often the reason that something succeeded or failed was mainly down to pure luck – especially the luck of fortunate or unfortunate timing.

Tobias Lütke, co-founder of Shopify, has openly credited much of his company's success to luck, specifically fortunate timing. He said, 'This is not the kind of company that could have been started two years later,' emphasizing that Shopify's rise benefited from the e-commerce boom.

Quibi was a short-form streaming platform that launched in April 2020. It was founded by Jeffrey Katzenberg and Meg Whitman and aimed to deliver 'quick bites' of premium content designed for on-the-go viewing on mobile devices. It attracted significant investment and high-profile talent, and generated considerable buzz.

Quibi's core value proposition – entertainment for busy people on the move – was severely undermined by the unforeseen and rapid onset of the Covid-19 pandemic. The pandemic led to widespread lockdowns and stay-at-home orders globally, drastically reducing commuting, travel and other activities where short-form mobile viewing would have been most appealing. Suddenly, people had more time and were primarily consuming entertainment at home on larger screens.

The pandemic accelerated the adoption of existing long-form streaming services like Netflix, Disney+ and Amazon Prime Video, which offered a vast library of content suitable for extended viewing periods at home. People were less inclined to pay for a separate service focused on short, mobile-first content when they were already well-served by these alternatives.

Chengwei Liu and Mark de Rond[6] explored the concept of luck and its implications in management and organizational behaviour. Their research showed that luck is often overlooked in favour of skill or effort when evaluating performance. This oversight can lead to attribution bias, where people mistakenly attribute success or failure to personal qualities rather than external factors like chance.

They found that people credit or blame themselves or others for results influenced by chance. One key finding was that people often misinterpret luck as skill, especially in high-performance situations. This misattribution can lead to overconfidence and flawed decision-making. Liu and de Rond argue that recognizing the role of luck can improve strategic thinking and decision-making by reducing biases.

A key element of luck is timing. A great idea at the wrong time will flounder. But luck can shape circumstance to favour the fortunate. In the late 1990s, the internet was booming and numerous search engines emerged (e.g. AltaVista, Yahoo! Search, Excite). Google, founded in 1998, entered a crowded market. However, it had the luck of timing. While Google's PageRank algorithm was undeniably innovative and a significant factor in its superior search results, its timing in relation to the dot-com bubble burst played a crucial role in its eventual dominance.

The dot-com crash of 2000–2001 devastated many early internet companies. Companies with unsustainable business models, heavy spending and a lack of profitability collapsed. Google, while also navigating the downturn, had a more sustainable approach. Crucially, it wasn't burdened by the legacy infrastructure and inflated valuations of some of its older competitors. As these competitors struggled or disappeared, Google, with its superior technology and relatively lean operations, was well-positioned to capture the growing search market as the internet recovered. While the founders' vision and engineering prowess were essential, the *timing* of the dot-com bust created a less competitive landscape, allowing Google's technology to shine through and gain significant market share without the intense competition it might have faced had the bubble not burst when it did. Many other promising search engines simply didn't survive to see the internet's full potential realized.

Here is another classic example of how a missed opportunity, potentially due to a confluence of factors including timing and misjudgement, can drastically alter the course of technological history. IBM chose Microsoft's fledgling operating system over Digital Research's established CP/M for the original IBM PC, a decision that was critical to Microsoft's success.

In 1980, IBM was developing its first personal computer, the IBM PC. It needed an operating system. Digital Research, led by Gary Kildall, had CP/M (Control Program/Monitor), which was the dominant operating system for microcomputers at the time. It was widely used and had a large library of existing software. Microsoft, co-founded by Bill Gates and Paul Allen, was a relatively small company primarily known for its BASIC programming language. It did not have its own fully fledged operating system for the Intel 8086/8088 architecture that the IBM PC would use.

The popular narrative suggests that when IBM representatives arrived to meet with Gary Kildall to discuss licensing CP/M, he was out flying his plane. While the specifics of this are debated, it's clear that the initial interactions between IBM and Digital Research did not lead to a deal quickly. Some accounts also mention that Kildall's wife, Dorothy McEwen, who handled the business side, was hesitant about IBM's initial terms, particularly regarding a non-disclosure agreement and the licensing model.

Digital Research reportedly wanted a per-copy royalty for CP/M, which was the company's standard practice. IBM, accustomed to different licensing models, preferred a one-time fee for unlimited use. This difference in business approach became a sticking point. The eventual price of CP/M-86 (the 16-bit version for the IBM PC) was significantly higher than PC-DOS, making it less attractive to consumers.

Digital Research was late in delivering the 16-bit version of CP/M (CP/M-86) that could run on the IBM PC's architecture. This delay gave Microsoft an opening.

When IBM's initial discussions with Digital Research stalled, Bill Gates and Microsoft stepped in. Although they didn't have a suitable operating system, they saw the immense potential of the IBM PC. Microsoft quickly acquired a rudimentary operating system called QDOS (Quick and Dirty Operating System), later renamed 86-DOS, from Seattle Computer Products for a relatively small sum. This OS was designed to be similar to CP/M. Microsoft adapted 86-DOS to the IBM PC's hardware and licensed it to IBM as PC-DOS. Crucially, Microsoft retained the right to license MS-DOS (the same OS under a different name) to other computer manufacturers, a strategic move that would prove incredibly lucrative as the 'IBM PC-compatible' market exploded. Microsoft offered attractive licensing terms to other PC makers, often on a 'per-machine' basis, which incentivized manufacturers to bundle MS-DOS with their clones, further solidifying Microsoft's dominance.

The IBM PC deal was a watershed moment for Microsoft. It catapulted the small language company into the forefront of the software industry and laid the foundation for its future dominance with MS-DOS and later Windows. Despite having a technically sound and initially dominant operating system, Digital Research gradually lost market share to MS-DOS. The missed opportunity with IBM had long-lasting consequences for the company. While it continued to innovate with products like DR-DOS, it never regained its leading position.

Had Digital Research secured the deal with IBM, the history of personal computing could have been very different. CP/M might have become the standard, and Microsoft's trajectory could have been significantly altered.

The story of Microsoft and Digital Research with the IBM PC is a powerful example of how timing, strategic decisions (or indecision) and even seemingly minor factors can have monumental consequences in the business world, especially in the fast-paced technology industry. Digital Research's inability to capitalize on the opportunity, for whatever combination of reasons, paved the way for Microsoft's unprecedented rise.[7,8]

Research suggests that career success can be attributed to about 50 per cent luck and 50 per cent hard work, while some studies assign as much as 55 per cent of the outcome to luck.[9]

Because we attribute results, whether good or bad, to our efforts rather than to our fortune, we underestimate the role of luck. This leads to those who have had business success being overconfident in their abilities and those who have had failures to be too hard on themselves. Instead, we should put success and failure behind us and be ready to seize good luck whenever it occurs.

Make your own luck

Richard Wiseman has studied why some people are lucky and others are not. In his book *The Luck Factor*, he advises that there are four main traits that lucky people have that help them to be 'lucky':

- They create, notice and act upon chance opportunities that come up.
- They make good decisions using their intuition as well as their logic.
- They have positive expectations about the future.
- They don't let bad luck get them down; they find a way to turn it into good fortune.[10]

By changing your attitudes, behaviours and actions, you can change your luck. If you see obstacles as opportunities rather than difficulties, then you can turn them to your advantage. If you notice unusual things and think laterally, you can see novel openings. This is particularly true in the contexts of creativity and innovation.

You can develop luck-promoting traits through deliberate practice. Start by putting yourself in new environments. Attend events outside your usual network, engage with people from different industries or backgrounds, and try new activities. Each fresh encounter increases the chances of stumbling upon something valuable.

When making decisions, balance logic with instinct. Write down both your initial gut feeling and your reasoning and review the results later. This builds your ability to blend data with intuitive judgement. See Chapter 23 on trusting your intuition.

Resilience is another cornerstone of luck. Reframing failure by asking 'What did I learn?' or 'What path might this lead to?' helps transform setbacks into stepping stones. Lucky people don't avoid failure – they learn how to mine it for future wins.

Can you change a corporate culture to be luckier? I believe that you can. Senior leaders and managers can foster luck. For example, they can promote opportunity scanning. Leaders can encourage a culture where team members are alert to emerging trends, customer feedback or unexpected events. A manager might set up regular 'opportunity-spotting' sessions where staff share unusual insights or market shifts they have noticed.

Organizations can also use structured tools like scenario planning or retrospective reviews to make sense of ambiguity and extract lessons from the unexpected. Innovation labs, trend reports and customer journey mapping are all methods that help employees think ahead and see connections that others might miss.

Cross-functional collaboration further enhances this effect. When people from different departments work together, they combine perspectives, uncover hidden opportunities and solve problems more creatively.

Leaders should tell stories about the importance of spotting and seizing opportunities. Show that decisions are often made with incomplete information. Leaders have to balance data and intuition and can encourage others to do so.

Above all, senior staff should display a positive expectation and mindset. Leaders who maintain optimism, even during organizational turbulence, can inspire teams to persevere and remain receptive to new possibilities. They can become luckier and help their people do the same.

Summary

Many people blame bad luck for their failures – especially in ventures where they invested considerable time and effort. People with a positive outlook recognize that each obstacle is a step along the way and that there is much that can be learned from setbacks. They learn lessons from reverses and they seek out fresh opportunities. They are always optimistic and receptive to ideas. They see opportunities in situations where others give up. They make their own good luck.

When the great golfer Gary Player was asked why he was so lucky, he replied, 'The harder I work, the luckier I get.' So the lessons are clear. There is a way to be lucky. It involves a positive attitude, hard work, observation, preparedness, action and a willingness to see every setback as a learning opportunity and a step towards success.

Questions

Looking back on your life and career, write down three of your biggest successes and two of your biggest failures. For each item assign a percentage for how much of the result you believe was down to luck and how much down to your efforts. Did luck play a bigger role than you previously assumed?.

08
Build a culture of experimentation

Booking.com runs over 25,000 tests every year. This approach has transformed a small startup into a giant of the travel industry. Extensive experimentation has been crucial for its marketing and innovation strategies.[11] According to Lukas Vermeer, Director of Experimentation, the company runs over 1,000 experiments at a time. It runs tests for individual website visitors to test specific ideas and learn what works better. These are mostly A/B tests, where the results are assessed from two alternatives. In this way the company can find an ideal sequence for each customer journey on its site.

How does Booking.com create this culture of experimentation? Stuart Frisby, who was Director of Design, set the guidelines. First, no HIPPOs (highest paid person's opinions) are allowed to dominate. Second, every decision is a democracy, but every decision is tested. Third, trust your tools.

Building a culture of experimentation within a business means that unexpected opportunities are stimulated and exploited. It can lead to groundbreaking innovations, improved processes and a workforce that is more engaged and adventurous.

How can this be achieved in practice?

Creating this type of culture starts with the leaders. Commitment across the leadership team is crucial in fostering a spirit of experimentation. Leaders should redefine what success and failure mean. They can encourage a growth mindset that accompanies a culture of experimentation. This involves creating an environment where employees feel empowered to share new ideas, test them and rapidly scale the winners. The leadership team should live this culture day in and day out to ensure the organization keeps pace in a rapidly changing business environment.

Employees should be empowered to test hypotheses and iterate with one trial after another. This means providing the time and the tools for experimentation together with encouragement to use them. By empowering everyone to test, organizations can drive innovation and prevent stagnation. This approach allows team members to become comfortable with trying out new ideas and applying a 'test and iterate' approach to their day-to-day activities. Some organizations allocate a specific amount of time each day for employees to pursue their interests and try out ideas. 3M famously allowed its researchers to spend 15 per cent of their time on investigating any scientific topic that caught their interest, regardless of whether or not it had a direct bearing on their job objectives.

Google encourages creativity by allowing all employees to spend 20 per cent of their time on side projects. This has led to many minor innovations and some major ones, including Gmail and AdSense. This approach applauds experimentation and allows employees to explore new ideas without fear of criticism. By encouraging creative exploration and making it an expected part of the job, organizations like Google and 3M can foster a culture of continuous trialling and innovation.[1]

Leaders of innovation encourage employees to take small bets and risk failure. They publicly praise the efforts of those who experiment, even if the results are failures. Some companies encourage staff to take risks by gamifying the process with rewards for experiments and ideas, regardless of the outcome. This approach can help combat the natural instinct to avoid failure and aims to encourage more experimentation.

Fostering many small bets has been crucial to Amazon's success. The company continually tests new styles, products and methods to see what works best for buyers and sellers. This worked wonders with Amazon Prime and the Kindle, but it has also led to many marketing disasters, including the Amazon Fire (a line of tablet computers) and Amazon Destinations (a hotel booking service).

Fostering processes for experimentation

What approach should you as leader adopt? First, provide employees with the time and resources they need to freely experiment with new techniques or to build something of their own. You do not have to be as generous as Google with its 20 per cent time for experiments – perhaps one day a month is enough. And the budget can be quite small to begin with.

Provide employees with the training and support they need to conduct experiments effectively. This can be done by offering workshops, webinars and other resources to help employees develop the skills and knowledge they need to experiment.

Use data to validate outcomes. Wherever possible, get people to document their experiments with data on the results. Many of the endeavours will be used to test ideas, for example whether customers would prefer a new approach. Sampling results and data need to be shared. Learn to thrive on data. Experiments have a purpose and that is to provide data that will test hypotheses. Adam Savage is a special effects designer, educator and television personality, best known as the co-host of the popular Australian TV series 'MythBusters'. He stated, 'In the spirit of science, there really is no such thing as a "failed experiment". Any test that yields valid data is a valid test.'[12] It is vital that we learn to use data to learn from each trial, whether it is initially labelled a success or a failure.

Consider gamifying the experimentation process by creating website tables for ideas submitted, experiments run or win rates of experiments. LabQuest has revolutionized how companies conduct experiments by integrating gamification into its testing approach. The platform transforms standard A/B testing and user research into games with points, badges and leaderboards. Participants earn rewards by completing tasks or giving feedback. This games-based approach has significantly increased participation rates and data quality. The company reports 72 per cent higher engagement and 40 per cent more useful insights compared with traditional methods.

Changing the culture

At the heart of experimentation lies a mindset, a willingness to be wrong, to learn and to evolve. Yet many organizations struggle not because they lack tools but because of fear of failure. People feel that they lack the permission to fail. Psychologists describe loss aversion as a tendency to fear losses more than we value gains. In business, this manifests as risk avoidance, perfectionism and decision paralysis.

To counter this, leaders must normalize failure as a learning mechanism. Amazon's Jeff Bezos famously said, 'If you know it's going to work, it's not an experiment.' This philosophy encourages bold bets, knowing that a few big wins will outweigh many small losses. Booking.com's Lukas Vermeer echoes this, noting that experiments aren't about proving someone right – they're about discovering what works.

A useful framework for experimentation is the Build–Measure–Learn loop, popularized by Eric Ries in *The Lean Startup*.[13] It starts with a clear hypothesis: 'We believe that changing X will improve Y.' Then comes the test – ideally small, fast and low-cost. Next, measure the impact using relevant metrics. Finally, learn from the results and decide whether to scale, tweak or abandon the idea.

This loop isn't just for product teams. HR can test new onboarding formats. Marketing can trial messaging variations. Even finance teams can experiment with budget-allocation models. The key is to treat every initiative as a learning opportunity, not a verdict.

Ethical experimentation is also crucial. When testing with real users, transparency matters. Inform participants, respect privacy and avoid manipulative tactics. A culture of trust strengthens the foundation for experimentation.

To embed this mindset, consider rituals such as 'Failure Fridays', where teams share what didn't work and what they learned. Or create an 'Experiment Wall' to showcase ongoing tests. These practices reinforce that experimentation is not a side activity, it is how progress happens.

Leaders need to create an environment where failure is seen as a natural part of the experimentation process. Encourage employees to share their failures and learn from them. This can be done by creating a safe space for employees to discuss their failures and brainstorm ways to improve.

Celebrate and reward successes – and failures! Praise people for both their successes and failures to reinforce the value of experimentation. Share the results. Publicly recognize employees who take risks and experiment, regardless of the outcome.

Steven Bartlett is the founder of social media marketing company Social Chain and the founder of *The Diary of a CEO* podcast. He stresses the importance of building a culture of experimentation. 'Get your team to conduct fast, fearless experiments – more often.' He added, 'Every Monday, my social team report to me a list of experiments that they did in the last seven days.' He also said, 'Your team either behave in that way or they don't, and that's usually, honestly, down to the leadership.'[14]

Summary

Airbnb conjectured that professionally photographed listings might perform better than user-uploaded ones. It ran a controlled experiment with professional photos for some listings and user-generated photos for others. The result was surprising. Listings with professional photos received two-and-a-half times as many bookings and earned hosts more than $1,000 more per month. This unexpected lift led Airbnb to launch a full-scale photography programme, transforming how hosts presented their properties.[15]

We need to run more experiments. Learn from Booking.com. We need to change our corporate culture to be more open, curious and experimental. We need to overcome the tendencies to be risk averse and to avoid appointing blame for failure. We need processes that enable and fund multiple tests and trials. Experiments will often lead to satisfying results that confirm your ideas and will often lead to disappointing results that negate your hypotheses. And sometimes they will lead to completely unexpected results and unexpected opportunities.

Ultimately, experimentation is not just a method, it's a philosophy of curiosity, humility and continuous improvement. Organizations that embrace it don't just adapt – they lead.

Questions

How many experiments have you or your team carried out in the last month? What hypothesis could you test tomorrow with one or more A/B tests? Plan now to run some experiments. You will learn things.

09
Ensure psychological safety

If you want people to find unexpected solutions, you have to make people feel comfortable with unexpected situations. People need psychological safety.

Amy Edmondson, a Harvard Business School professor, pioneered the concept of psychological safety in workplace environments. She defines this condition as a shared belief that the team environment is safe for interpersonal risk-taking. It creates an environment where people know that they can speak up without fear of humiliation or punishment. Edmondson's research demonstrated that psychological safety is an essential basis for experimentation, learning and innovation.

In her research in the 1990s she found that high-performing teams spoke openly about mistakes. Lower-performing teams kept quiet about mistakes and missed the opportunity to learn from them.

In a psychologically safe culture, people feel able to express radical ideas, ask questions, give constructive feedback and admit mistakes without fear of criticism or negative consequences. It goes further than a broad level of trust because it directly allows people to admit vulnerability in communications at work.

Psychological safety serves as the foundation for innovative environments. When team members feel secure, they openly acknowledge mistakes, creating valuable learning opportunities rather than repeating failures. This safety empowers people to voice unconventional ideas that otherwise might remain hidden. Teams can engage in healthy debate, exploring diverse perspectives without damaging relationships. Since innovation inherently involves uncertainty, psychological safety provides the space for calculated risk-taking without the fear of blame. When people don't fear judgement, they freely share knowledge and expertise, fostering a richer collective intelligence that fuels creative solutions.

Creating psychological safety in organizations

Edmondson recommends several practical approaches for leaders. She says that managers should frame challenges as opportunities for growth rather than tests of competence. It is important to acknowledge uncertainty and complexity in the work.

Leaders could admit their own mistakes and the painful lessons they have learned in their careers. By showing their own vulnerability, they signal that failure is part of the process and imperfection is acceptable. Furthermore, how leaders react to mistakes powerfully shapes psychological safety. They can send a powerful message by avoiding public criticism and instead treating failures as learning opportunities rather than reasons for punishment.

Innovative organizations use various processes, such as brainstorms and open forums, to gather ideas and feedback. In these, the leaders ask questions and demonstrate genuine interest in team members' perspectives. They clearly show that diverse viewpoints are valued.

Research shows that psychological safety delivers significant business benefits. Edmondson's studies show that teams in an environment with psychological safety outperform teams with more conventional attitudes to blame and mistakes. This is particularly true where there are complex tasks requiring creativity and collaboration.

People who feel psychologically safe show higher commitment and engagement. This leads to better talent retention. Moreover, by sharing more information, especially on learnings from mistakes, teams can make better decisions and react faster to change. They are better able to handle the unexpected.

Candour

A prime example of a company employing these methods is Pixar. In his book *Creativity Inc.*, Ed Catmull, president of Pixar Animation and Disney Animation, explains the important role of the 'braintrust' in the creative success of Pixar.[16]

He starts by stressing the importance of candour. It is essential for open and honest discussion. The opposite of candour is reserve and there are many reasons why people should be reserved. When you are fresh into a company and go to a meeting, it is only natural to be polite, show respect, defer to authority, try to avoid embarrassment and avoid looking like an idiot. These are all good reasons to be reserved and hold off making critical comments. It is also the case that strong and confident people in meetings can intimidate others and can easily signal that they do not like criticism. Catmull argues that we need to be aware of all these factors and others that mitigate against candour. We should show by words and actions that candour is wanted and appreciated.

At Pixar this process was initiated by stressing to staff that 'early on, all our movies suck'. A key part of the initiative to innovate and improve movies is what Pixar calls its 'braintrust'. This is a group of people whose job it is to review the plans, progress, storyboards and early reels of each project at regular intervals. The braintrust group includes experienced people with deep understanding of movies and audiences. They give the project director clear spoken feedback on what they like, what works, what doesn't work and what they think is a problem. They do not prescribe solutions, fixes or ideas and they have no authority to mandate changes. How to fix the issues raised is the responsibility of the project director and their creative team.

The role of the braintrust group is advisory. It is benevolent, it wants to help and has no other agenda. The film itself is under the microscope, not the director. As Catmull puts it, 'You are NOT your idea.' If there is an argument, it is there to excavate the truth. No one tries to win. Interestingly, the forceful character Steve Jobs was never invited to join a braintrust meeting.

Why is this necessary? Because every movie director becomes lost in their project. They become immersed in the detail. Where once they saw the forest, they can now only see the trees.

Catmull draws this analogy. Pixar is a hospital. The movie is a patient. The director is the doctor in charge. The braintrust is a group of other doctors and experienced clinicians. They ask questions and add their ideas. They are striving to find out what is wrong with the patient and help them to recover.

Nevertheless, even with all these good intentions and practices in place, Catmull found that he had to continually strive to eliminate the barriers to candour in the meetings and across the company.

Very few organizations operate at the high level of creativity needed at Pixar where every project is a clever, innovative and original animation. But every organization has projects, systems and practices that need candid feedback. We all need to find ways to increase candour.

Overcoming a blame culture

A culture that lacks psychological safety is one in which people are blamed for their failures and mistakes. This is highly damaging for learning, improvement and innovation. If people are worried that the finger will be pointed at them for trying things that don't work, then they will not try them. And if people are scared of recriminations, they will not own up to errors and mistakes, which means that an opportunity for improvement and learning is missed.

This problem is particularly acute in the healthcare sector where a blame culture can discourage whistleblowers and individuals who want to report errors – their own or those made by others.

The *Daily Telegraph* newspaper reported that in 2002 Gary Kaplan, Chief Executive of the Virginia Mason hospital in Seattle, visited a Toyota factory in Japan where he was surprised to see first hand the company's remarkable 'stop the line' philosophy.[17] Any worker on the multimillion-pound production line can stop the line if they experience an unexpected problem or difficulty. Senior technicians and managers rush over – not to berate the worker but to help them and to learn. That way they can improve the process for all workers and all Toyota plants. It is all part of the company's famous 'kaizen' or continuous improvement concept.

Dr Kaplan wanted to introduce a similar process at the hospital so that staff would immediately report any incident which could be harmful to a patient. But he ran into opposition. The existing culture was ingrained. People did not want to go over the heads of doctors or report things that might get colleagues into trouble. Doctors feared that admitting mistakes might lead to lawsuits.

It took a dramatic accident in November 2004 to trigger the change. A 69-year-old mother of four died after she was injected with the wrong medication. The hospital immediately issued an apology and took full responsibility.

It made staff realize that Kaplan's policies were designed to save patients and not to chastise staff. There are now about 800 safety reports at the hospital every month, revealing everything from tiny defects to major mix-ups. The reports are acted upon with the aim of improving the process so that such mistakes cannot occur again. Blame and fear have been replaced with learning and improvement. The result is that Virginia Mason is now recognized as one of the safest hospitals in the US. Remarkably, the change to an 'owning up' culture has led to a 75 per cent reduction in lawsuits and a corresponding reduction in the cost of liability insurance premiums.

Two pertinent lessons for innovative leaders are clear from the story of Dr Kaplan and his hospital. First, a great way to innovate is to copy an idea from an entirely different field – in this case automobile assembly. Second, corporate cultures are remarkably resistant to change and it often takes dramatic actions to alter them.

We can also learn from the remarkable improvements in the safety record of the aircraft industry. After every major plane crash there is a detailed investigation – not to assign blame but to learn what went wrong and to determine how the faults in process, equipment or procedure can be eliminated. The lessons are shared with all airlines and aircraft manufacturers.

If you have a blame culture in your organization and you want to change it to one of transparency and honesty, here are some practical steps you can take:

- Focus the message on the benefits of innovation and continuous improvement and on the risks inherent in covering up failures. Senior executives and managers should lead the way by pointing out mistakes they have made and how similar errors can be avoided in the future.
- Whistle-blowers who point out serious flaws and failings should be singled out for praise (unless they wish to remain anonymous).
- You could invite an external speaker from an entirely different industry (e.g. Toyota) to tell their story.

Summary

If you want unexpected innovation, then building a culture of psychological safety and candour is essential. People need to feel comfortable expressing unorthodox ideas and suggestions. Many organizations do the opposite. They have allowed an atmosphere of blame to develop and this makes people risk averse. It takes a determined effort on the part of leaders to change this. Kaplan's example at Virginia Mason hospital shows how it can be done. Transparency and openness will shine a spotlight on reckless or incompetent individuals. But that is not its primary purpose, which is to enable continuous improvement based on all the little fears, problems and errors that clog the current systems and stop us from being more efficient and more innovative.

Questions

Think about a large organization that you have worked for or know well. Does the organization ensure psychological safety? Can people say what they want, within reason, without fear of criticism? Could a whistle-blower carry an important concern to a senior executive? Is there an atmosphere of candour?

10
See what others miss

Observation is a critical yet often underappreciated skill, particularly in business. It is more than simply looking. It is seeing what others miss. Observation is the careful act of noticing, understanding and exploiting the subtle things that most people overlook. In business, we are busy and overloaded with information. If we can find the ability to observe, it can give us a crucial advantage. We will look at some research into observation and see why people miss critical details. We will look at how you can foster observation in yourself and your team.

There is much evidence that we are not very good at noticing things around us. Psychologist Richard Wiseman carried out an experiment on observation. He asked people to go through a newspaper and count how many photographs it contained. The participants were diligent in counting the pictures – some went through the paper twice, just to be sure. None of them noticed the headline on the second page which read, 'There are forty-two pictures in this newspaper.' They also completely missed an advert in the paper which said, 'Stop counting and tell the experiment leader that you have seen this to win £100.' They were too busy focusing on the task to observe these opportunities.

A famous study known as the 'Invisible Gorilla' experiment showed how people can miss obvious events when focused on a particular task. Participants were asked to watch a video of a basketball match and count the number of passes. They failed to notice a man in a gorilla suit who walked across the court. This illustrates how selective attention can blind us to the unexpected – a risk in business settings where tunnel vision can lead to missed threats or opportunities. You can see the video on YouTube if you search for 'Invisible Gorilla'.

Attention focused on a task can cause us to miss important signals around us. This is known as 'inattentional blindness'. There are many experiments showing that when people are focused on a specific task, they may completely miss unexpected changes or opportunities right in front of them.

Observation is more than just noticing things; it is a device for gathering knowledge and spotting opportunities. In business, observation skills are valuable because they can uncover hidden faults, inefficiencies or customer needs. Observation can reveal emerging trends that are not yet obvious in the data. Business leaders who deliberately observe customers, staff and competitors can make better decisions and lead innovation.

Furthermore, observation can trigger our imagination and creativity. A team at Amsterdam University led by psychological scientist Matthijs Baas studied links between observation skills and creativity.[18] Results showed that strong observation skills were linked to greater creativity, originality and flexible thinking.

Why are we so poor at observation? Excessive focus on the task at hand is one reason. Complacency and routine are also culprits. As we become increasingly familiar with routine, we stop noticing anomalies and changes. We can also fall victim to cognitive biases. We just see what we expect to see and are blind to information that does not fit our assumptions.

Observing customers

It is good to ask customers questions but it is better to observe them in action. Many companies conduct conventional customer surveys and focus groups. These are useful channels of feedback, but in terms of original ideas they are often disappointing. Customers are good at demanding incremental improvements in products, lower prices and better service, but they are notoriously poor at predicting significant new products or innovations to meet their needs. Which wearer of spectacles in the 1950s would have said that he wanted a lens to put on his eyeball or laser surgery to reshape his eye? You can expect customers to tell you that they want more of what you offer and they want it better, faster and cheaper. But do not count on them to tell you about different ways to meet their needs.

A more lateral approach to gain insights from customers is to study in detail how they use your type of product or service and to observe what practical problems they have.

Haier is a leading Chinese manufacturer of white goods such as freezers and cookers. Its engineers in rural China were surprised to find that people were using Haier washing machines to wash the vegetables they had grown in their gardens. Turning this unexpected use into a new application, the Haier development team came up with a new wash cycle designed specifically for vegetables.

On another occasion a sharp-eyed engineer saw that a student had placed a plank between two Haier fridges to form a makeshift desk. The company responded by designing a fridge with a fold-out desktop – ideal for small rooms that need an extra table or desktop.

When Levi Strauss & Co observed its customers, it noticed that some of them deliberately shrank their jeans to get a tighter fit and others deliberately ripped them. So Levi's brought out lines of pre-shrunk jeans and pre-ripped jeans.

Asking customers for feedback is good, but observing them can be much better. If you want to gain a march on the competition and design the products and services of the future, watch your customers carefully. Look for the areas of unexpected use, the headaches and problems that need to be solved or the unusual combinations of needs or uses. These can give you the insights you need to generate successful innovations in products, services and processes.

Positive deviants

Positive deviance (PD) is an idea which is based on the observed principle that in any community there are people who adopt unexpected and successful approaches to problems that beset the whole community. These people are the 'positive deviants'.

The PD approach was developed by Jerry and Monique Sternin with the charity Save the Children in Vietnam in the 1990s. Researchers worked in villages where 64 per cent of children were malnourished. They observed that some villagers, though no better off than their peers, had children who were well-nourished. These families had developed different behaviours and tactics, including gathering foods which others disdained (e.g. sweet potato greens, snails and crabs).

It is known that rural communities often react badly to external experts telling them what to do. These people prefer to learn from each other. So Jerry and Monique developed a nutrition programme based on the practices of the positive deviants. Participants were encouraged to attend classes with the new foods and fellow villagers showed them how to cook them. After two years of the programme malnutrition had declined by 85 per cent.

The key principles of the positive deviance approach are:

- Communities already have the solutions – they are the best experts to solve their problems.

- Communities self-organize and have the human resources and social assets to solve an agreed-upon problem.
- Collective intelligence and know-how are not concentrated in the leadership of a community alone or among external experts but are distributed throughout the community.
- Sustainability is the cornerstone of the approach.
- It is easier to change behaviour by practising it rather than just knowing about it.

The PD approach has been applied in countries around the world.

The concept has spread to business. In every large organization there are some people who find more effective ways of getting things done – often by bypassing rules and obstacles that impede the majority. The trick is to find these people and then use PD approaches to roll out the innovations. The process generally looks like this:

1 Identify a common problem area in the business.
2 Identify positive deviants – people who have found ways around the problem.
3 Capture their methods and ideas.
4 Design a programme to inform and motivate others to use the formulae of the PDs.
5 Run a pilot workshop to test the programme.
6 Roll out to the whole community and embed the new behaviours.

A core principle of PD is that the best way to change behaviour is through actions. It is easier to act your way into a new way of thinking than think your way into a new way of acting. So giving lectures and writing papers on how people should change is much less effective than finding a way to persuade them to try the change.

Every business has challenges and problems – including some chronic issues that the executive team has struggled to solve. But according to Monique Sternin, 'The solutions to seemingly intractable problems already exist – probably in plain sight.' You just have to find the positive deviants.

Actions we can take to boost observation

There are various exercises we can undertake to boost active listening.

- We need to pay attention to what is said and how it is said.
- We must learn to watch out for non-verbal cues.
- How often during conversations do you find yourself not listening to what the other person is saying? Perhaps you are thinking about what you will say next.
- Minimize distractions during conversations by silencing your phone.

- Do not interrupt the other person but let them finish.
- Develop your open-ended questioning technique by resisting the temptation to give an instant answer. Instead ask a question such as, 'Can you give me more detail?' or 'What are your ideas here?' or 'How do you feel about this?'
- We need to develop our attention to detail. Concentrate on the present moment and avoid multi-tasking. Try to notice inconsistencies, patterns or small changes that could signal larger issues or opportunities.

It is important to be present. Focus fully on the moment, whether in meetings or one-on-one interactions. Seek feedback from others to gain different perspectives and check your observations.

It can be helpful to keep a journal of the things you notice. List small observations that you spot throughout the day. For example, you might write down things that seem odd or out of place, feelings that you experience and unexpected things that people say or do. Occasionally browse through your journal for insights and ideas.

Leadership and observation

Many great leaders have been noted for their observational skills. Apple's Steve Jobs was famous for his attention to detail and his ability to anticipate customer needs before they were articulated. He observed users' frustrations with existing technology and this led him to develop the graphical user interface in the Macintosh personal computers and later intuitive products like the iPad and iPhone.

Ingvar Kamprad, the founder of Ikea, was renowned for his use of observational research to understand his customers. By closely watching customer movements and interactions, Ikea was able to redesign its store layouts to maximize engagement and sales. For instance, the company found that only about 20 per cent of customer purchases were planned; the rest were prompted by the in-store experience. This insight led to Ikea's 'Gruen effect', which encourages impulse buying by guiding customers through a carefully designed path filled with visual stimuli and intriguing items.

Leaders who are good observers watch out for emerging trends in customer behaviour and for subtle shifts in the dynamics of their teams. They are better able to make timely course corrections, unlock opportunities and build high-performing teams.

American businessman Howard Schultz observed the social role of coffee shops in Italy. He deduced that there was an unmet need for something similar in America. He founded Starbucks to provide a 'third place' between home and work. His company went on to become a global café experience.

Summary

The art of observation is a crucial skill in business. Sherlock Holmes said, 'You see, but you do not observe.'

We need to understand the difference between seeing and observing. We need to develop observational skills in what we see, what we hear and what we sense. The ability to notice what others miss can mean the difference between success and failure. By cultivating observation skills, leaders can anticipate and exploit unexpected opportunities, avoid costly mistakes and stay ahead of the competition.

> ### Questions
>
> Try keeping an observation journal for a week. What unexpected or unusual things do you notice? Keep your eyes peeled for curious occurrences. Note at least six items each day and at the end of the week read through the list to see what ideas and actions are spurred.

11
Exploit mistakes

In January 1992 a container with 29,000 plastic bath toys was washed overboard in the Pacific Ocean. The toys were manufactured in China and were en route to the US. They were called Floatees, bath toys consisting of red beavers, green frogs, blue turtles and yellow ducks. Unlike many bath toys, these had no holes in them, so they did not take on water. At some stage the container broke open and the toys were released. Another ecological calamity!

An oceanographer based in Seattle, Curtis Ebbesmeyer, learned of this event and saw it as a singular opportunity to study ocean currents. He and his partner, James Ingraham, set out to track the toys. A typical oceanographic study would release 500–1000 drift bottles, of which only 2 per cent might be returned. So a sample of 29,000 items represented a significantly bigger and more accurate experiment. Ebbesmeyer alerted beachcombers, marine scientists and coastal workers to be on the lookout for the distinctive toys. Sure enough, 10 months after the consignment was lost at sea, the first rubber ducks washed up in Alaska. Over the next 20 years the ducks turned up in all sorts of places. Some washed up in British Columbia and Hawaii, some got stuck in the Arctic ice, many others circumnavigated the globe.

Each reported recovery was entered into a computer program which models ocean surface currents. The study of where and when the ducks made landfall helped increase understanding of gyres, persistent ocean currents. For example, the North Atlantic gyre is a huge circular current that passes the US east coast, Western Europe and Africa. It takes about three years for a piece of flotsam to go once around the gyre. The work of Ebbesmeyer and Ingraham helps us understand how flotsam moves around the world's oceans and thus can assist in plans to tackle the pressing problem of marine plastic waste.

Every time there is a calamity or when things go wrong, the pieces on the board are disturbed. That means that there are new possibilities. Disasters can open the door for innovations. It just needs a little lateral thinking.

In 1903, French chemist Édouard Bénédictus accidentally dropped a glass flask coated with cellulose nitrate. To his surprise, the glass cracked but didn't shatter. The inner coating had held the shards together. Recognizing its potential, Bénédictus developed laminated safety glass by sandwiching a plastic layer between two sheets of glass. Initially used in gas masks during World War I, it later became standard in car windshields and building materials. This accidental discovery significantly improved safety in transportation and architecture, preventing countless injuries from shattered glass. A simple lab mishap led to a life-saving innovation.

Every mishap, mistake and failure tells us something we did not know before. Sometimes we can harness this lesson into an unexpected solution. In 1957 Alfred Fielding and Marc Chavannes tried to create a fashionable new form of insulated wall covering by sealing together two shower curtains. The trapped air bubbles made bad wallpaper. It was a flop – nobody wanted it. They tried selling it as greenhouse insulation – it failed again. Then IBM needed something to protect its new computers during shipping. The computers were expensive and fragile. A new form of packaging was required.

Fielding and Chavannes started a company, Sealed Air Corporation. It promoted their new product, which they called bubble wrap, and IBM was one of their first customers. Packaging companies quickly embraced the new technology. Previously, the best way to protect an item during shipping was to surround it with balled-up newspaper, but that was messy, dirty and did not offer great protection. Bubble wrap became a huge success.

How do we achieve this in practice?

The fear of failure can inhibit progress, yet history gives us many examples in which mistakes became the stepping stones to groundbreaking innovation. Shifting our perspective from viewing mistakes as terminal setbacks to valuable learning opportunities is crucial for fostering a culture of innovation. Here are some ways that we transform failures into advantages.

Start with a growth mindset. Cultivating a growth mindset, as popularized by American psychologist Carol Dweck,[19] involves believing that abilities and intelligence can be developed through dedication and hard work. When failures occur, focus on the lessons learned rather than dwelling on the perceived mistakes. Ask, 'What can I learn from this?' rather than, 'Why did this happen to me?'

British inventor James Dyson developed more than 5,000 vacuum cleaner prototypes, most of which failed. This ultimately led to the creation of his revolutionary bagless vacuum cleaner. He viewed each failure as input in a learning process. He refined his design with each iteration.

After a failure, conduct a thorough post-mortem, a business analysis to identify the root causes of the failure. This involves open and honest discussions to pinpoint what went wrong and how it can be avoided in the future. The '5 Whys' method is a simple but powerful technique for uncovering the root cause of a problem. In repeatedly asking 'Why?' (usually five times), each answer forms the basis of the next question, helping you to dig beneath surface issues to expose deeper, underlying causes that might otherwise go unnoticed. Use this and other questioning methods to systematically dissect the failure. Then document the findings and share them across the organization.

The best example of post-mortem analysis is the aviation industry's rigorous post-crash investigations. They have drastically improved air safety. Each crash is thoroughly investigated and the results are shared with authorities, airlines and manufacturers to improve safety. Every incident yields valuable data that leads to design improvements and procedural changes.

As mentioned previously, psychological safety is essential. It is the belief among your people that they will not be punished or humiliated for speaking up with ideas, questions, concerns or mistakes. Encourage open communication and transparency. Create an environment where employees feel comfortable taking calculated risks and sharing their failures without fear of reprisal.

'Project Aristotle' was a research initiative conducted by Google to determine what makes teams effective. The project's findings significantly impacted how companies understand and approach teamwork. The research found that psychological safety was the most crucial factor. Teams with high psychological safety are more likely to learn from their mistakes. They experiment, innovate, collaborate and perform well.

Undertake iterative experimentation and product development. Products should be continuously refined based on feedback and failures. Be in 'perpetual beta', testing prototypes with a handful of customers. Be prepared to change direction when necessary. Adopt agile methodologies and rapid prototyping to quickly test ideas and gather feedback. Encourage experimentation and be willing to abandon failing projects.

Slack started as a gaming company called Tiny Speck. When the game failed to gain traction, the company realized the internal communication tool it had developed was far more valuable. It pivoted and Slack became a billion-dollar company.

Finally, I would recommend creating a system for documenting and sharing lessons learned from failures. This knowledge base can prevent future mistakes and foster a culture of continuous improvement. Develop internal databases, case studies or workshops to disseminate information about failures and the resulting insights.

NASA has extensive documentation of past missions, including failures like the Apollo 13 incident, when an oxygen tank explosion led to the famous words, 'Houston, we have a problem.' This documentation serves as a valuable resource for future space exploration endeavours as learnings are used to prevent similar errors.

By adopting these strategies, organizations can transform failures from roadblocks into springboards for innovation, driving progress and creating a culture of continuous learning.

Summary

Mistakes and failures are learning opportunities. First, we must achieve a culture of psychological safety and candour where people can openly talk about mistakes and failures. Then we need to use the questioning methods discussed in earlier chapters. Failures should be analysed as a learning and sharing exercise. We should always be on the lookout for unexpected insights that come from failures and be ready to act on them.

Questions

List some of the mistakes and failures you have experienced in the past 12 months. If you cannot think of any mistakes, it shows that you have not been adventurous enough! For each slip-up, analyse what you could have done differently and what lessons you have learned. Did any misstep yield an unexpected benefit? Who do you know well enough to discuss some of these issues with to share learnings?

12
Turn obstacles into opportunities

Reed Hastings was annoyed when he was charged a $40 fee for returning a DVD six weeks late at Blockbuster. He reasoned that many other people also would be annoyed by the problem of late returns and this insight gave him the inspiration to found Netflix and change the way people consumed films and video.

In business and in our personal lives, obstacles, irritations and difficulties can appear as infuriating barriers to progress. However, history has demonstrated that these challenges can become unexpected stimuli for innovation and clever solutions. The trick is to change our perspective and to reframe obstacles as opportunities.

In Tim Harford's book *Messy*[20] he tells a story of American jazz pianist Keith Jarrett who in 1975 was booked to give a concert in Cologne, Germany. Jarrett arrived on the day of the concert and was shocked to find that the piano provided was not the concert model he had ordered. It was small, old, out of tune and some notes did not work. He told the organizer that he could not perform the concert with that damaged piano. No other was available and an audience of 1,400 people was due to arrive that evening. The organizer implored him to play so Jarrett reluctantly agreed. He had to adapt to the inadequate instrument and he did so brilliantly. The album of the concert proved remarkably popular, selling 3.5 million copies. As Harford says, 'He produced the performance of a lifetime, but the shortcomings of the piano actually helped him.'

Overcoming obstacles requires resilience and adaptability. It helps us develop mental fortitude, flexibility and self-confidence. Furthermore, overcoming difficult obstacles can lead to groundbreaking innovations. When faced with limitations, we are pushed to think creatively and find alternative solutions. This is the principle behind the old saying 'necessity is the mother of invention'. Let's look at some practical examples.

At the end of the first Gulf War in 1991, fires were raging out of control in the Kuwaiti oil refineries. What could be used to put them out? A lateral solution was found. The pipelines that were normally used to pump oil from the refineries to the ports were used to pump water to the refineries. By using an existing resource and reversing the flow, the problem was overcome.

When faced with impediments, our initial reaction is often frustration or dejection. However, if we choose a growth mindset, we can transform these obstacles into stepping stones to success. We should see them not as insurmountable barriers but as invitations to innovate and even as resources to exploit.

In 2008, during the global financial crisis, roommates Brian Chesky and Joe Gebbia were struggling to pay their rent in San Francisco. This financial obstacle drove them to find an innovative way to make money. It became the inspiration for Airbnb. They started to rent out air mattresses in their living room during a design conference when hotels were fully booked. Surprisingly, it worked. This creative solution to their personal financial challenge evolved into a global platform that revolutionized travel accommodation, a business that is now valued at billions of dollars. The key obstacle, financial hardship, became the trigger for a business model that would fundamentally transform the hospitality and travel industries.

It is not just inventors who use these creative problem-solving techniques. Governments and state bodies are generally risk averse, but sometimes they are presented with a problem which causes them to try something radical. In 2005 the IRA (Irish Republican Army) pulled off a major robbery at the Northern Bank in Belfast – they got away with £25 million in banknotes. How could the authorities catch the criminals or stop them using the proceeds of their crime? They came up with a clever idea using one of the resources within the problem – the stolen banknotes. They changed the bank notes in Northern Ireland and reprinted all the bills. Anyone holding old bank notes had to bring them in to be changed – and that is a big problem if you are holding millions of stolen banknotes.

More recently, the Covid-19 pandemic presented an unprecedented challenge to businesses worldwide. However, this obstacle catalysed a dramatic shift in work culture. Technologies like Zoom, Slack and Microsoft Teams seized this opportunity to provide seamless communication tools. Traditional businesses also adapted, embracing remote work cultures. This shift not only reduced companies' overheads costs, it also expanded global talent pools and improved employee satisfaction.

How do we achieve this?

By changing our approach, we can try to turn obstacles into prompts for innovation. Stop cursing obstacles as problems. Instead reframe the challenge by viewing them as benefactors sent to help you. Deliberately view them as opportunities for growth and innovation. List possible advantages that the obstacle might bring. Ask yourself, 'How can I use this as a resource?' or 'What different approach can we try here that will lead to improvement?'

Jürgen Klinsmann was a talented German football player who moved to England to play for Tottenham Hotspur in 1994. Initially he was unpopular with fans because he had a reputation for 'diving' – faking a foul in order to win a free kick or penalty. He cleverly turned this around. After he scored a great goal, he did a funny dive onto the pitch in a parody of himself. From then on, whenever he or his team-mates scored a goal, they did the dive and fans loved it – and him.

Focus on what you can control. This approach allows you to take constructive action rather than feeling overwhelmed by circumstances beyond your influence.

Sometimes when there is more than one problem, consider using one issue to solve another. When prolific inventor Hiram Maxim went pigeon shooting, he noticed two problems. One was the strong recoil of the rifle into his shoulder. The second was that he had to stop to reload the gun. In using the force from the recoil of a bullet to load the next bullet, he invented the machine gun. He turned the problem into the source of the innovation.

I recommend that you embrace experimentation and be prepared to pivot. Cultivate a mindset of flexibility and openness to change. Run more experiments. If you can pivot around an obstacle while your competitors are continuing to face it with traditional methods, you have an opportunity to steal a march on them.

Summary

Turning obstacles into opportunities is not always easy. It requires courage, experimentation, speed and adaptability. Not all experiments will work, but each stumble is a learning experience. By viewing challenges as catalysts for growth and innovation, individuals and organizations can unlock fresh potential and achieve remarkable outcomes. Some of the significant advances and successful pivots in business have emerged from what initially appeared to be insurmountable obstacles. Companies that manage to do this boost employee morale, enhance their reputations and increase their resilience and ability to face future challenges.

Here is one final story to add to the ones above. Oprah Winfrey was working as a local TV news anchor in Baltimore when she was moved to co-host a morning talk show called 'People Are Talking'. She and the people around her saw this as a demotion and almost a punishment. Nevertheless, Oprah persevered in the new role and discovered her natural talent for connecting with guests and audiences. It became the foundation for her remarkable success in popular media.

> **Questions**
>
> Think of a major obstacle that is inhibiting progress in a project at work or in your personal life. Write it down. Express it as clearly as you can. Can you list four ways in which you could you use this obstacle for your advantage? It helps if some of the ways are rather silly or even absurd. Ponder what you have written and let your mind turn over some possibilities.

13
Unexpected actions in marketing

So far in this book we have looked at unexpected events, meetings and actions that happen to people often by chance. But there is a different kind of unexpected action – one deliberately designed to catch competitors off guard and surprise the market.

The classic example of the deliberate unexpected action to outsmart opponents was the Trojan Horse. In Greek mythology, when the Greeks laid siege to the city of Troy, they found they could not overcome its formidable defences. They therefore withdrew their armies to signal that they had given up, leaving the gift of a giant wooden horse, which the credulous Trojans took through their gates and defences. Of course, it was trap and the soldiers concealed within the structure soon emerged to lay waste to the city. The expression 'Trojan Horse' has since become a metaphor for all manner of cunning and deceptive attacks.

Let's review some examples of unexpected business actions or strategies which challenged conventional thinking and helped organizations steal a march on competitors.

A surprising move which revolutionized an industry was electric car maker Tesla's action in bypassing the traditional dealership network. Instead of relying on franchised dealers, Tesla established its own showrooms and online platform. Elon Musk's company chose to sell directly to consumers. This approach gave Tesla greater control over pricing, customer experience and brand messaging. Tesla eliminated the middleman and streamlined the buying process. It could offer fixed pricing and a no-haggle environment, which was a clear contrast to the wrangled prices at dealerships. This direct model also facilitated a closer relationship with customers, allowing for direct contact and feedback.

Most unexpected marketing initiatives do not set out to transform the market. They are often designed to make a strong short-term PR impact. Their surprise value can garner precious media coverage.

Examples

In 2012, energy drink company Red Bull sponsored Felix Baumgartner's record-breaking freefall jump from the edge of space. This thrilling live event captured global attention, perfectly embodying Red Bull's brand ethos of extreme adventure and energy. The stunt generated extensive media coverage and social media buzz that boosted the brand's visibility far beyond traditional advertising. The marketing executives at Coca-Cola and PepsiCo must have been astonished.

In 2007, rock band Radiohead released their new album, *In Rainbows*, using a 'pay what you want' pricing model. Instead of a conventional fixed cost, fans were invited to pay whatever they felt the album was worth. This surprising move generated enormous media coverage and built goodwill with customers. It redefined how artists could engage directly with their audiences on value, challenging the industry norms of music pricing and distribution.

Patagonia's 'Don't Buy This Jacket' campaign was a bold and unexpected marketing strategy that encouraged customers to think twice before making a purchase. Launched on Black Friday 2011, the campaign featured a full-page ad in *The New York Times* with the headline 'Don't Buy This Jacket' above an image of the company's popular R2 fleece jacket. The advert highlighted the environmental cost of production and urged consumers to consider the environmental impact of their purchasing decisions. By promoting this approach towards responsible consumption, Patagonia reinforced its brand image of being committed to environmental sustainability.

There are many examples of unexpected advertising campaigns that took risks to get the message across. For instance, the Old Spice 'The Man Your Man Could Smell Like' campaign. This aftershave brand had been seen as stuffy and outdated. Old Spice underwent a radical reinvention with its humorous and daring 'The Man Your Man Could Smell Like' campaign. The TV commercial featuring Isaiah Mustafa on a horse was released in

February 2010 and gained widespread attention during the Super Bowl that year. The offbeat ads caught viewers by surprise and shifted public perception. Old Spice was transformed into a fun, modern brand that resonated with younger customers. Sales were revitalized.

Some companies deliberately set out to outrage with audacious actions. The news that unauthorized horse meat had been found in various parts of the European meat trade in early 2013 caused a major scandal. Consumers and regulators were up in arms. Paddy Power, the Irish online gambling company, seized the moment by issuing with its annual results a 36-page cookbook of horse-meat recipes. The recipe book had the subtitle 'From Stable to Table'. This deliberately outrageous campaign gained significant publicity. Ken Robertson, Paddy Power's 'head of mischief', said, 'We wanted to reflect our brand persona as a mischief-maker.'

On 1 April 1998 Burger King published a full-page advertisement in *USA Today* announcing an innovative new product, the 'Left-Handed Whopper'. The ad stated that the new Whopper had the same ingredients as the original Whopper. However, the Left-Handed Whopper had 'all condiments rotated 180 degrees'. The resulting benefit for left-handers was that most of the condiments would 'skew to the left, thereby reducing the amount of lettuce and other toppings from spilling out the right side of the burger'.

Jim Watkins, senior vice president for marketing at Burger King, claimed that the new sandwich was the 'ultimate "HAVE IT YOUR WAY" for left-handed customers'. The next day Burger King issued a follow-up press release revealing that the Left-Handed Whopper was a hoax and that thousands of customers had gone into restaurants to request the new item. Meanwhile, many others requested their own 'right-handed' version.

This hoax generated considerable media coverage and goodwill for Burger King. It is listed as one of the best all-time April Fool's jokes. In this case Burger King did not just rotate its product by 180 degrees – it rotated its marketing and communication to a similar extent and with great results.

How to generate unexpected initiatives

These kinds of surprising stunts and clever schemes can only flourish in a climate that is comfortable with adventure, risk and failure. Leaders need to employ creative and unorthodox thinkers and give them the freedom to try their crazy ideas. They have to instruct their agencies to be bolder. Each of the examples above carried considerable risk; there are countless lesser-known examples that flopped.

I recommend that you assemble a diverse group of smart people in a brainstorming meeting and ask them to come up with audacious ideas. They will. Start with some provocative questions, such as:

- How can we surprise and delight customers?
- How can we shock the competition?

- How can we gain massive media coverage?
- What market assumption or rule can we break?

Encourage people to initially come up with bizarre or even absurd ideas. If you start with a ridiculous idea, it can probably be adapted to form a creative idea. If you start with a reasonable idea, it will probably turn into something bland and unexciting.

At first the team will generate many ideas without any judgement or criticism. You then discuss and review the ideas with constructive comments. Eventually the team can select a shortlist of the most promising concepts. Now you need to figure out how you can quietly test the idea. Be warned that if you go through the whole process, generate some great ideas and implement none of them, then the exercise will prove disappointing and demotivational for the staff. It takes courageous leadership to give the go-ahead to bold and risky ideas – but fortune favours the brave.

Summary

Marketing is a fertile field for unexpected actions. It is a place where David can overcome Goliath by clever, impudent or risky actions that capture attention. You have to be prepared to roll the dice. There is always a danger that a campaign will flop, or that some people will be upset or offended. Bland marketing upsets no one but engages no one and is remembered by no one. Sometimes it is worth deliberately doing the unexpected to gain awareness and competitive advantage.

> **Questions**
>
> Could any of the organizations that you have worked for have carried out an audacious marketing campaign or clever stunt? Could they have done what Patagonia or Burger King did? Have you ever worked for a courageous leader who let their people take significant risks in the marketplace? Could you if you were in that position?

14
Work in diverse fields

Polymaths

Erez Lieberman Aiden was born in Brooklyn in 1980. He is a polymath. He is a mathematician, engineer, biologist, physicist, historian, computer scientist and linguist. He is a professor of molecular and human genetics at the Baylor College of Medicine, in Houston, Texas, and formerly a fellow at the Harvard Society of Fellows, in Cambridge, Massachusetts. He is an adjunct professor of computer science at Rice University, in Houston.

Around 2005 he was trying to solve the problem of how to sequence the human immune system. He could not crack the issue. Then he happened to attend a conference on immunology and wandered into the wrong lecture. While sitting there he had a brilliant idea to help solve a different problem: how to find the three-dimensional shape of the human genome. Something in the talk stimulated him to combine ideas from maths and physics to come up with the idea.

Aiden's ability to draw from multiple scientific domains enabled him to tackle the intricate problem of genome structure. An unplanned moment can yield valuable opportunities, and in this case it fostered a connection between different disciplines. Delving into diverse fields and ideas, even inadvertently, can stimulate innovative thinking and problem-solving.

Leonardo da Vinci excelled in art, science, engineering, anatomy and mathematics. Galileo studied astronomy, physics, engineering, philosophy and mathematics. Benjamin Franklin's interests included politics, diplomacy, science and inventing. Nikola Tesla was an inventor whose skills encompassed engineering, physics, maths and futurism.

You do not have to be a genius to harness skills in diverse fields. We can modestly emulate Aiden and da Vinci by deliberately studying different disciplines and acquiring varied skills. Read and research in areas which are not closely linked to your core expertise. Develop a wide curiosity for all sorts of ideas, whether in science, engineering, design, music or entertainment. Ideas from one field can lead to surprising ideas in others.

Research by Robert Root-Bernstein, a professor of physiology at Michigan State University, and his colleagues shows that polymaths are creative because they integrate ideas from diverse fields. Root-Bernstein says that creativity is not confined to a single domain but is enhanced by combining disparate ideas, skills and knowledge. He argues that although a creative work such as a song, a sculpture or a scientific theory sits in its own domain, the mental processes that lead to the generation of creative ideas are the same wherever. So, we find that many innovative scientists have hobbies in arts or music and that some of the most innovative artists and musicians have an interest in the sciences. Brian May, the lead guitarist of Queen, is a polymath. He is admired by rock fans for his innovative guitar techniques and compositions. May holds a PhD in astrophysics, showing a blend of artistic and scientific prowess.

Being a polymath can significantly enhance creativity and problem-solving abilities. A multidisciplinary approach helps develop a cognitive flexibility that is invaluable in both personal and professional contexts. There are several ways that this might work.

People working on multiple different projects often find that one project can somehow cross-fertilize another. The polymath's broad knowledge base allows them to draw connections between seemingly unrelated fields. This can lead them to find solutions that specialists in just one field might miss. For example, the National Stadium, also known as the Bird's Nest, in Beijing, China was designed by Swiss architecture firm Herzog & de Meuron. The company won a competition which had 13 finalists for the design of the stadium for the 2008 Olympic Games. Their design drew on ideas from Chinese ceramics and nature – creating the iconic bird's nest appearance. The eminent Chinese artist Ai Weiwei was the artistic consultant on the project.

People working on multiple projects in different fields often find that when they get stuck on one project and then turn to another, their unconscious mind is still working on the first tough problem. There are many stories of ideas that suddenly arrived while the person was walking or was in the shower.

Another advantage is that polymaths can deploy a wide array of tools and methodologies from different disciplines. When faced with a challenge in one field, they can sometimes draw on a technique they learned in another. For example, someone expert in psychology and engineering might be able to design technology which is more user-friendly because it addresses both technical and human factors.

Hedy Lamarr was an Austrian actress and star of many films in the 1930s and 1940s. She was described as the most beautiful woman in the world. But many of her admiring fans did not know that she was a polymath. She spoke four languages, was a pianist, dancer and film producer. She was also a scientist. In 1946 she founded her own production company. In collaboration with the avant-garde composer George Antheil, she invented an electronic device that minimized the jamming of radio signals. This device is a component of present-day satellite and cellular phone technology.

Intersections

Serendipitous discoveries with unexpected benefits can occur in the intersection of different disciplines. German physicist Wilhelm Conrad Röntgen discovered X-rays while experimenting with cathode rays. He noticed that a fluorescent screen in his lab started to glow even though it was not in the direct path of the rays, leading to the discovery of a new type of radiation. This accidental discovery in physics had a transformative impact in medicine.

Another happy confluence happened between electronic engineering and medicine. While working on a device to study heart rhythms, American engineer Wilson Greatbatch accidentally installed the wrong resistor in a circuit, leading to the discovery of a pulse that could regulate the heartbeat, resulting in the development of the implantable pacemaker.

Liquid crystals represent a state of matter which exists between solid and liquid states. They were discovered in 1888 by Austrian botanist Friedrich Reinitzer, who was studying cholesterol at the Charles University in Prague. Reinitzer described three important features of cholesteric liquid crystals: the existence of two melting points, the reflection of polarized light and the ability to rotate the polarization direction of light. These discoveries remained of academic interest only until they were put to practical use some 80 years later when teams at RCA Labs and Kent State in the US independently created early liquid crystal displays by manipulating the crystals with electrical charges. The displays first appeared in digital clocks and watches, but in 1984 LCD resolution improved to the point where it could display images instead of mere text, allowing computer makers to create lightweight laptops and displays.

The unexpected element in this story is that a botanist discovered something that is now a key part of computer technology. The concept was developed into a product by physicists and engineers. It is at the intersection of the sciences that some of the greatest innovations happen.

Steve Jobs is often regarded as a visionary who worked at the intersection of technology and graphic design. His approach to product development at Apple was based on marrying advanced technology with sleek, user-friendly design. Jobs pushed for an intuitive and visually appealing user interface, which led to the development of the graphical user interface (GUI) for the Macintosh. Jobs had a keen interest in typography, which he learned about during a calligraphy class. This influenced the inclusion of multiple fonts and advanced typographic features in the Macintosh, setting new standards for personal computers. By focusing on the intersection of technology and design, Steve Jobs helped to create products like the iPhone which are functional but also beautiful and easy to use.

Summary

Being expert in different fields can significantly enhance creativity and problem-solving abilities. The diverse knowledge base, cognitive flexibility, cross-pollination of ideas and improved problem-solving skills are all valuable assets for the problem-solver. The polymath is more likely to find unexpected solutions because they are wandering through different worlds that stimulate unusual ideas. Leonardo da Vinci, Hedy Lamarr and Steve Jobs were all exceptional people, but if we can learn a little from their approach, it is to work in diverse fields and develop varied skills.

> **Questions**
>
> Can you develop your polymath abilities? Have you ever found that you got an unexpected idea for one problem while working on another? If you are working on a project that is giving you headaches, try putting it on the back burner. Devote your energies to something that uses your brain in a different way – maybe building a wall, playing the piano or learning a language. You might find that your unconscious mind does the heavy lifting in the background and gives you the ideas you need.

15
Seize the unexpected opportunity

Günter Schabowski was a politician and spokesman for the government of the East German state (the GDR). On 9 November 1989, he was assigned the task of addressing a press conference with West Germans as well as local reporters. He had been given a slip of paper with details on a new policy on border crossings between East and West Germany. At the end of what had been a dull conference, something unexpected happened. Schabowski casually read out the first part of the report. He mistakenly declared that people could cross the border prematurely and without visas. The border policy was intended to come into effect the next day, once administrators had had time to get themselves and the relevant paperwork organized. Schabowski seemed to announce the immediate end of the Berlin Wall. The news raced around Germany and the world. That night massive crowds gathered at the wall, which was forced to open after dividing the city for 28 years. Soon afterwards, the entire border opened. This led to the fall of the East German regime and to German reunification.

People rushed to the border to seize on an opportunity that resulted from an error. They played a key role in the start of the end of the Cold War, which led to global ramifications. When something unexpected happens, don't get annoyed, get curious. Ask yourself what unexpected benefits this anomaly might bring.

Stephanie Kwolek (1923–2014) was a Polish-American chemist who worked for DuPont Corporation for 40 years. In 1965 she was working on developing a lightweight yet strong fibre for use in tyres. During her experiments with polyamides under low-temperature conditions, she created a solution that was unusually thin and cloudy, unlike typical polymer solutions. This sort of cloudy solution was usually thrown away. Instead of discarding it, however, she became curious and insisted on testing it. She was told not to use the spinneret machine because it was thought the solution would clog the machine. However, Kwolek persuaded her colleague to let her use the spinneret to test her solution. She was amazed to find that the new fibre would not break when nylon typically would. Her discovery led to the development of Kevlar, which is five times stronger than steel by weight and has since been used in a wide range of applications. Kwolek's work has had a significant impact on both industrial materials and personal safety equipment, saving countless lives through its use in bulletproof vests alone.

Tips at a corporate level

It is essential to quickly assess the potential value and possibilities in a surprising experimental result. Kwolek knew she had developed something remarkably strong. She could not anticipate that it would have so many valuable uses, but she knew the discovery had great value.

The next step is to develop an action plan to test feasibility and opportunity. Resources must be allocated and supported. Once senior DuPont managers were informed of the discovery of the new material, they immediately assigned a group to work on it. They immediately saw great potential, but they could not have foreseen that Kevlar would today have more than 200 applications, including tennis rackets, skis, parachute lines, boats, aircraft, ropes, cables, tyres, hockey sticks and armoured cars.

A large research organization like DuPont has a culture of encouraging creativity, experimentation and risk-taking. It has systems and processes that allow for quick decision-making. It allocates people and money to develop promising ideas. It rewards employees for identifying and pursuing unexpected opportunities. Conventional businesses need to borrow some of these cultures and processes. They need to adopt a research and development mindset – but with an emphasis on speed and simplicity. They need to rapidly test assumptions and hypotheses.

The minimum viable product

A great way to test a promising new product idea is with a minimal viable product (MVP). Eric Ries introduced the concept of the minimal viable product and explains it in his book, *The Lean Startup*.[21] The MVP is a rudimentary version of a new product that has just enough features to show to a limited set of customers in order to gain feedback for product development. The primary goal of an MVP is to test the basic hypotheses of a new product and gather insights with small cost and few resources.

The idea is to start the learning process as soon as possible. Critically, this approach helps companies avoid building products that customers do not want. By showing and gaining reaction to core functionalities, businesses can iterate. They can refine their offerings based on real user data and feedback rather than assumptions.

To use the MVP approach, start by identifying the core problem your product aims to solve and the key features required to address this problem. Develop a simple version of the product that includes these essential features and launch it to a small segment of your target market. Collect feedback through direct interactions, surveys or usage analytics and use this information to make informed decisions about future iterations.

The MVP approach encourages a cycle of continuous improvement and innovation, allowing businesses to adapt to market demands efficiently. It emphasizes the importance of learning in the development process, helping companies to pivot or persevere with confidence based on empirical evidence.

Viagra

The discovery of Viagra by Pfizer is a classic example of serendipity in pharmaceutical research. Initially, scientists at Pfizer were researching a compound called sildenafil citrate as a potential treatment for cardiovascular issues, specifically hypertension and angina pectoris. During clinical trials in the early 1990s, researchers noticed an unexpected side effect: many male participants experienced significant penile erections. This observation led Pfizer to pivot the focus of sildenafil's development.

Recognizing the potential of this side effect, Pfizer decided to market the drug for erectile dysfunction, a condition that previously had received little attention in medical research. The company patented sildenafil in 1996 and rapidly moved it through clinical trials specifically targeting erectile dysfunction.

Pfizer capitalized on this opportunity through a bold marketing campaign that included direct-to-consumer advertising, which was relatively novel for prescription medications at the time. The company also engaged high-profile figures, such as former presidential candidate Bob Dole, to publicly endorse the drug, which helped destigmatize erectile dysfunction and boosted Viagra's popularity. This aggressive marketing strategy, combined with the drug's effectiveness, led to Viagra becoming a cultural phenomenon and a commercial success, generating billions in revenue for Pfizer.

Despite the eventual expiration of its patent and the introduction of generic versions, Viagra remains one of the most well-known pharmaceutical products worldwide. It shows how an accidental discovery can be developed into a major commercial success.

Tips at a personal level

We can learn many lessons from entrepreneurs who seized unexpected opportunities. Here are some tips for spotting and acting on these windfalls.

Pay attention to your frustrations and complaints. Many innovative ideas emerge from problems you encounter personally. When you catch yourself saying 'I wish there was a better way to...' or 'Why doesn't anyone make...', take note. These frustrations often signal market gap frustrations that others share but haven't addressed. Travis Kalanick and Garrett Camp, successful tech entrepreneurs, were attending a tech conference in Paris in 2008 when they couldn't get a taxi. Standing and waiting, they were frustrated about being unable to hail a cab. They started complaining about how inefficient and unreliable traditional taxi systems were. This led to them asking, 'Why can't we just push a button and have a car come to us?' This moment of frustration became the seed for Uber, which revolutionized urban mobility worldwide.

Cultivate genuine curiosity about a broad range of interests. As we have seen, unexpected opportunities often come from the intersection of different industries or disciplines. Stay curious about fields outside your expertise, attend diverse events and read broadly. Cross-pollination of ideas can lead to innovative solutions.

Develop a bias towards action over analysis. When you spot a potential opportunity, resist the urge to research it to death. Set a short deadline for initial exploration, then take a small, low-risk step to test your hypothesis. Speed often matters more than perfection when opportunities are emerging. Sara Blakely was selling fax machines door-to-door when she cut the feet off her tights to create a smoother look under her white trousers. This moment of frustration led her to develop the idea for Spanx. She invested her $5,000 in savings in the venture and built a billion-dollar shapewear business.

Build relationships before you need them. Opportunities often come through people, not systems. Maintain genuine connections across different industries and levels of seniority. The person who tells you about an unexpected opening or partnership might be someone you helped years ago or met at a random event.

Train yourself to see problems as potential goldmines. When something breaks, fails or disappoints you, ask 'What if this could be done completely differently?' instead of just accepting the status quo. The biggest opportunities often hide behind the most accepted inconveniences.

Maintain your financial and professional flexibility. Unexpected opportunities often require quick pivots or initial investments. Maintain some savings, avoid over-committing your time, and structure your life so you can take calculated risks when the right moment presents itself. Flexibility is your gateway to seizing opportunities others can't pursue.

The key is developing a recognition of opportunity while maintaining the courage to act when others hesitate.

Summary

It is important to remain open to and prepared for the unexpected. Strange things will happen. Most of them are inconvenient or irrelevant, but occasionally something happens that signals a significant opportunity. You need to be ready to hear that signal. It is highly beneficial in life to cultivate a mindset that is receptive to serendipity. When something unexpected happens and you hear the signal, take action. Just like the people in East Berlin who heard a fumbled announcement from a government official. They tested the new possibility and pushed their way across the border, leading to the fall of the Berlin Wall.

Large companies like DuPont and Pfizer are geared up to seize opportunities for innovation, whether these happen by design or by chance. Small organizations with fewer resources must find ways to do some of the same. If you cannot afford to put a strong development team on the case, then try the smallest viable product you can produce to test the idea. Spot the idea, assess its potential and then test it. Seize the moment.

Questions

How many unexpected opportunities have you seized in the last year? How about in your life as a whole? Can you look back and say, 'Thank heavens I chose to do that'? Was there something lucky or unexpected that led up to that decision?

16
Why do we not seize opportunities?

Most of us will have experienced serendipity at some time in our personal or professional lives. Maybe luck or circumstance presented you with a golden opportunity. Did you take it? If yes, well done. If not, why not?

In this chapter we will explore the common barriers to recognizing and seizing opportunities. Why do we often fail to take up openings or grab lucky breaks? Let's consider three main causes.

Prejudices

The word prejudice comes from the Latin, meaning to judge in advance. Prejudices are preconceived opinions that are not based on reason. We all suffer from prejudices to some extent or other. They can cloud our judgement and prevent us from seeing the potential in others or in certain situations. We tend to like ideas from people we like and dislike ideas from people or sources we dislike. Many people like ideas that conform to their view of the world and dislike those that challenge it. Would you discard an unexpected idea if it came from a source you did not respect?

There are numerous historical examples where leaders or decision-makers ignored valuable ideas or contributions due to personal disdain or prejudice against the individuals proposing them.

Geneticist Barbara McClintock discovered transposons, or 'jumping genes', which are DNA sequences that can change their position within a genome. Her pioneering work was initially ignored and met with scepticism by her male colleagues. It was only years later that the significance of her discovery was recognized. She was awarded the Nobel Prize in Physiology or Medicine in 1983. Evelyn Fox Keller wrote a biography of McClintock entitled *A Feeling for the Organism*.[22] In it she says that McClintock felt like an outsider within her field, mainly because she was a woman. And ironically, this enabled her to look at her scientific subjects from a perspective different from the dominant one, leading to important insights.

Alfred Wegener proposed the theory of continental drift in the early 20th century, suggesting that the continents were slowly drifting apart. His ideas were met with disbelief and disdain by the geological community. This was mainly because he was not a geologist by training but a meteorologist. It took decades after his death for the theory to gain acceptance and for plate tectonics to become a cornerstone of modern geology.

Srinivasa Ramanujan was a brilliant but self-taught mathematical genius from India. He faced significant scepticism when he first sent his work to prominent mathematicians in England. Many dismissed his work due to his lack of formal training and his status as an Indian outsider to the academic community. It was only through the active support of fellow mathematician G. H. Hardy that his contributions to mathematical analysis, number theory and infinite series were eventually acknowledged.

How can you identify and overcome your personal prejudices and those of the society around you? Start with intense self-reflection. Examine your beliefs and attitudes. Where do these come from? Are they based on facts or stereotypes? In particular, think about situations where you might have felt uncomfortable or biased against someone or something. Reflect on why you felt that way.

Ask for input. Sometimes, others can see our biases more clearly than we can. Ask friends, family or colleagues for candid feedback on your behaviour and attitudes. Listen carefully and do not argue, though it can help to ask for examples.

Engage with people from diverse backgrounds and ask them about their experiences and perspectives.

Critically analyse the newspapers, magazines and internet media you consume for underlying biases or stereotypes. Try to engage with media that represents a wide range of voices and perspectives. Deliberately choose papers and magazines that challenge your preferred views or politics. This can help challenge and broaden your viewpoints.

By actively working to identify and overcome personal prejudices, you can become a more balanced and objective individual. Similarly, once you are aware of societal prejudices, you can contribute to creating a more just and equitable environment in which diverse viewpoints are welcomed.

Bias

Bias can stop people from taking advantage of opportunities because it leads them to reject information that does not conform to their beliefs. Confirmation bias means that we selectively seek, interpret and remember information in a way that confirms our existing beliefs, even if those beliefs are flawed. This can lead to poor decision-making, missed insights and a general resistance to change or new ideas.

For example, consider a CEO who is convinced their new product idea is the 'next big thing'. Confirmation bias might lead them to direct their team to conduct market research that will confirm their ideas and to ignore or downplay data that suggests the product might not be successful. This might well lead to a costly product launch that fails to meet market demand. When an unexpected opportunity arises, this CEO might miss it because it does not sit well with their view of the world. They will look for reasons to find fault with or just dismiss the idea.

Xerox PARC invented many of the technologies that would later become integral to personal computing, such as the graphical user interface. However, Xerox's management suffered from confirmation bias, believing that their core business in copiers was their primary opportunity. This bias prevented them from capitalizing on their innovations, allowing companies like Apple to seize the opportunity.

In essence, confirmation bias makes us less open to new information, less likely to critically evaluate our assumptions and more prone to reinforcing existing patterns of thinking. This can be a significant barrier to recognizing and seizing new opportunities.

Procrastination

Perhaps the single most significant barrier to the implementation of new ideas is putting things off. Approximately 20 per cent of adults worldwide identify themselves as chronic procrastinators. The tendency to delay tasks really isn't just a personal quirk, it's a global phenomenon. Research suggests that procrastination costs businesses billions of dollars annually in lost productivity.

There is a phenomenon known as 'Student Syndrome'. It affects not just students but people in all walks of life. This syndrome involves the commencement of a task at the last possible moment before the deadline, despite having ample time to complete it earlier. It is a classic example of procrastination.

The search for perfection can easily lead to procrastination. Because we cannot conceive an ideal solution, we keep searching and searching. In most situations in life, there is a time for thought and a time for action. Here are some tips for overcoming the roadblock of procrastination.

If you are stuck in a rut, ask yourself why this has happened. Are you baffled by the problem? Are you scared of taking action? Are you lazy? Are you waiting for perfection? Are you worried about the costs or risks of taking action? Is there something in your mood or emotions that is holding you back? Be ruthlessly honest with yourself. Write down the reasons for your procrastination and you will see that most of them are feeble excuses. Focus on the serious issues and find ways to overcome them. Solve this problem the same way you solve other problems – with critical analysis and creative thinking.

Sometimes we have to admit to ourselves that it is all right not to know the answer. We cannot be right all the time and we cannot know everything. It is better to acknowledge that we do not have the solution right now and to move forward on that basis than to wait eternally for the correct solution to appear.

The perfect can be the enemy of the good. If we keep searching for the perfect partner, the perfect house, the perfect job, we might find that life has passed us by. We can strive for perfection, but we must recognize that although the journey is worthwhile, we will never arrive at the destination. Constant improvement is generally a better goal than outright perfection. If we are moving in the right direction then we will get somewhere useful. There is a saying that is used to inspire writers: 'Don't get it right, get it written.' It means that it is better to start writing and then correct and improve what you have done than to wait until you have completed all the research and planning you can possibly do.

Write down the benefits that will flow from completing the task. Perhaps it will help your finances, your prestige, your career, your relationships, your family, your social life, your health, your self-esteem. Each benefit is a reason for action. Follow this up with a list of the consequences if you fail to complete the task. Who suffers? How would you feel? Many people are more motivated by avoiding risks and negative consequences than by the rewards of achievement, so look at it both ways.

There are times when it is very difficult if not impossible to make the right decision. Under these circumstances you have two major options. You can keep analysing, keep thinking, keep talking, look for more information and wait to see if things become clearer. Or you can deliberately take some action, see what happens and then revisit the decision. One question that can help you when faced with these two options is this: 'What is the worst that can happen if I take this action?' If there is a risk that you could lose your job, ruin your relationship or start a war, then the action is almost certainly unwise. If the risk is manageable, then you should consider action rather than inaction. Doing something produces momentum – it gives you a different view of the situation and injects some energy. The important thing is to watch what happens and be prepared to change direction if necessary.

Finally, a great way to overcome procrastination is to articulate your goals. Break them down into manageable targets and write them down. Once we have told someone we are going to do something, we are more likely to do it. The sense of commitment and obligation is higher. Share your goals and targets with someone supportive. Sometimes they can be a partner in the activity. It is easier to go jogging in all weathers if you and your neighbour have a regular commitment to jog together. Share your goals and achievements. Celebrate every small success. It will keep you motivated.

Summary

There are many reasons why we do not seize the breaks that serendipity or circumstance present to us. Prejudices, bias and procrastination are all likely causes. It is said that at the end of our lives we are more likely to regret the opportunities that we failed to take than the mistakes and wrong decisions that we did make. Time for some self-reflection.

> ### Questions
>
> Think of two opportunities that you missed. Why did you not grab the chance? What caused your hesitation? Write down the main reasons for each missed opportunity and then analyse those reasons. Would you take a similar opening if it happened today?

17
Recognize hidden patterns

Can you develop the ability to spot trends before others do? Great business innovators often appear to have anticipated a trend. It seems they must have been prescient in that they got into the right place at the right time and produced the product or service that people wanted next.

How can some people forecast the future and anticipate the unknown while most of us only see the wave when it is already over us? The reality is more often that the innovators do not foresee the unknown; more likely they observe something that is already happening and see an opportunity in it. Science fiction author William Gibson said, 'The future has already happened, it is just unevenly distributed.'

What a minority of people are doing today the majority will be doing tomorrow. All you have to do is to find that minority. To do that you need to develop your skills at understanding trends. You can achieve this by keeping an open mind and trawling many different inputs. Search the internet. Read blogs. Scan different magazines. Travel to other countries. Meet new people. Discover things outside your normal zone of expertise and interest. Study innovative companies in your sector but look overseas – what is happening in Holland or Denmark or Singapore or India? Clever people there are already ahead of the game, so copy some of their great ideas.

There are massive competitive advantages in business for those that can spot trends early and act on them. Apple and Samsung saw the power and future popularity of touch screens for portable phones. The previous market leaders Nokia and RIM (maker of the BlackBerry) did not. Netflix saw the trend towards streaming and downloads while Blockbuster stuck with physical media like DVDs and was eclipsed.

There is a common misconception that brilliant ideas are based on sudden revelations and eureka moments. Great innovators are always on the lookout. They carefully assess small signals that others dismiss as noise. They are watchful for early signs of change.

Early identification of positive trends can lead to innovations, new business opportunities and competitive advantage. Early identification of negative trends can prevent losses or help you pivot. Kodak was an early pioneer of the digital camera, but it was unable to pivot. It failed to fully embrace the digital revolution, clinging to its film business. It needed a long-term plan. Early trend recognition should inform strategic plans for both individuals and organizations. Companies that do not consider scenarios for the impact of trends like artificial intelligence and robotics risk being left behind.

Cultivate pattern recognition skills

How can you develop skills in spotting new trends? It starts with active observation. We have to move beyond passive consumption of all the information around us into a state of deliberate observation. This is challenging when we are deluged with news, data, input and opinions from many sources. We need to be selective and constantly watchful for things that are at odds with the conventional. We need to look out for the unorthodox.

At the same time, you should broaden your inputs. Gather numerical and quantitative data from market research, sales figures, web analysis, demographic data and science reports. Gather qualitative input from conversations, anecdotes, customer feedback and even office gossip. Look beyond obvious sources. Survey fringe communities, niche publications, academic research and startups in your market. The volume of structured and unstructured data can feel overwhelming – the challenge is to make sense of it all and to be able to spot what is really pertinent.

The artful trend spotter embraces continuous learning from many sources. They challenge assumptions because they are aware of the exceptions to every rule. They like interdisciplinary thinking so that they can gather input from different angles and disciplines.

Alan Turing and the Enigma machine

One of the most celebrated cases of pattern detection concerns British military intelligence. During World War II, mathematician and computer scientist Alan Turing and his colleagues at Bletchley Park, the centre of Allied codebreaking during the war, cracked the German Enigma code by identifying patterns in encrypted enemy military communications. The Enigma machine used complex rotor settings that changed daily, making decryption seem impossible. However, Turing and his team searched for patterns and exploited weaknesses in how messages were structured.

An important insight was that no letter could be encrypted as itself, which eliminated possibilities and narrowed down the potential settings of the machine. Another key breakthrough was recognizing that German messages often contained predictable phrases, such as 'Heil Hitler' or weather reports. By analysing repeated letter sequences, the team developed a method which helped narrow down possible settings. Turing then designed the Bombe, an electromechanical device that rapidly tested Enigma configurations to find the correct key. By 1941, the team could decrypt German naval communications, helping Allied forces evade U-boat attacks. Their work shortened World War II by an estimated 2–4 years and saved countless lives.

Imagine that your customers are sending out coded signals. How can you crack the code? First you must listen to their messages. Second, look for anomalies or things that are unusual or repeated. Once you have a theory, test the hypothesis by asking questions and gaining feedback from customers.

Secondary consequences

Major changes, whether technological, regulatory or societal, often lead to unexpected consequences. Whenever you see a new trend, ask yourself what this might mean. What might be the unanticipated results?

- The invention of the motorcar meant that people could travel faster. A secondary effect was that people lived further from their place of work and the suburbs expanded. This meant more business for housebuilders.
- The lightbulb replaced candles. It also replaced going to bed early. Now people could read books or go out in the evening on streets and to buildings that were well lit. Theatres and booksellers benefited.
- The internet linked computers together. Jeff Bezos saw that this meant that people could buy things much more easily and he launched Amazon. Pierre Omidyar saw that it enabled communities to join together in auctions and he launched eBay.
- Social media sites like Facebook and Instagram were created to connect people and sell advertising. Their dramatic spread has led to serious concerns about privacy, scams, misinformation spread and mental health issues.

- The invention of plastic created a brilliantly flexible new material which revolutionized manufacturing and packaging. Its durability and low cost proved a boon. However, because plastic is not biodegradable, we have seen a huge impact in litter and pollution in the seas and on land. This has created opportunities for those making and using reusable packaging.
- The smartphone revolution led to unexpected industries, such as mobile gaming – consider Angry Birds or Candy Crush. It enabled a world of innovative apps – for example, Uber and Lyft in transportation, which operate as platforms that connect passengers with drivers through their mobile applications.

For each new trend there will be follow-ons, consequences and changes that create opportunities and threats. Every time that you see a change in your business world, play a little game of 'What if?'. What if this becomes a big trend? What will the consequences be?

Summary

Pattern recognition is a learnable skill, not just a rare talent. The process starts with an open-minded attitude and a willingness to listen out for weak or unusual signals. It is a continuous journey because trend spotting is an ongoing process in a rapidly changing world. Actively cultivate your observational skills and embrace intellectual curiosity. If you can spot new trends and consequent opportunities, it can lead to a competitive edge in both your personal and professional lives.

> ## Questions
>
> Spend a few moments speculating on what future trends might apply in your industry or sector. Try to go beyond the obvious to something that might be subtle or hidden. Who are the early adopters in your field who could indicate future trends? Are you spending time talking to them about how they see the future?

18
Unexpected outcomes in the arts

Throughout history, the arts have been transformed not only by deliberate genius but also by chance encounters, accidental discoveries, and unforeseen events. These serendipitous moments have propelled artists, musicians, writers and painters to new approaches, leading sometimes to masterpieces that might never have been conceived without a stroke of luck.

Art

One of the most famous instances of serendipity in painting came in 1872 with Claude Monet's 'Impression, Sunrise'. Monet was experimenting with different brushstrokes and colour mixtures to capture light and atmosphere when an accidental smudge led to a hazy scene of early morning in Le Havre, France. The painting's fresh, loose style was initially criticized but later hailed as a revolutionary step in the development of Impressionism.

Creating conditions for such chance moments involves fostering an environment of experimentation, patience and openness. Artists who work outside their comfort zone, with diverse materials and conditions, can enable accidental effects to evolve naturally. Imperfections and unplanned effects can lead to unexpected outcomes.

American artist Jackson Pollock stumbled onto his signature 'drip' style by accident. While working on a piece laid flat on the ground, paint spilled and splattered. Rather than discard it, he played with it. This dripping and splashing method became a new technique of abstract expressionism. The spill wasn't cleaned, it was exploited. Pollock turned a mess into a movement.

In filmmaking, many remarkable shots and visual effects have been discovered by accident. For example, the 'Vertigo Effect' in Alfred Hitchcock's film *Vertigo* was created unintentionally during filming. Early filmmakers accidentally discovered the slow-motion effect when they tried projecting film at different speeds.

Michael Jackson reportedly developed his iconic dance move, the Moonwalk, by accident while rehearsing for a performance.

Literature

The idea for Mary Shelley's *Frankenstein* emerged during a storytelling challenge among friends on a stormy night in Geneva. The goal was to write a ghost story, but Mary Shelley's vision, sparked by a vivid dream and discussions with Percy Shelley and Lord Byron, evolved into a new genre: science fiction. This was serendipitous because had the weather been pleasant, the story might never have been written. A thunderstorm gave birth to a new type of fiction.

The creation of Sherlock Holmes was a stroke of serendipity. In 1877 a young medical student, Arthur Conan Doyle, met a professor at the University of Edinburgh, Dr Joseph Bell. Dr Bell was a master of observation, possessing an uncanny ability to deduce a patient's profession, origin and ailments before a word was spoken. As Bell's student, Doyle was profoundly impressed by Bell's diagnostic skills and powers of deduction. Years later, when he wanted to create a unique detective character, Doyle drew upon his memory of Bell. He modelled Holmes's keen eye and powers of logical deduction on his former mentor.

At a much more modest level, my first book, *Lateral Thinking Puzzlers*, followed a chance meeting on holiday with a family who were keen lateral puzzle enthusiasts. We swapped stories. Later I looked for a book on the topic and could not find one. So, I submitted a collection of such puzzles to a number of publishers. Sterling Publishing accepted my manuscript and the book went on to be a bestseller.

Writers who want to encourage serendipitous outcomes should meet diverse and unusual people. They should explore outside their genre, mixing ideas from philosophy to science, comics to poetry. They should try altered states of mind, as some authors find breakthroughs during walks, sleep or emotional upheaval. Serendipity often lurks in discomfort, chaos or quiet moments of reflection.

Music

In music, one of the most renowned instances of a surprising outcome was The Beatles' discovery of the feedback effect during recording sessions in 1964. Paul McCartney accidentally hit an electric guitar string in a way that produced a sustained, harmonic sound, which became a new musical technique. This accidental discovery influenced future music genres such as psychedelic rock. McCartney also famously dreamt the melody for 'Yesterday'. He woke with the tune in his head, unsure whether he'd unconsciously plagiarized it. For weeks, he played it for people, asking, 'Have you heard this before?' Eventually, he realized the melody was original, gifted by a dream.

Musicians can create conditions for such breakthroughs by encouraging improvisation, experimenting with unconventional instruments or sounds, and allowing room for mistakes. Sound engineers and artists can foster a studio environment where experimentation is valued over perfection, creating space for chance to lead to inventive musical techniques.

Summary

Serendipity has played an invaluable role across all creative disciplines, often leading to revolutionary innovations and celebrated masterpieces – from Monet's loose brushstrokes and Shelley's monster to The Beatles' feedback effect and Pollock's drip paintings. These examples prove that not all discoveries are meticulously planned. By cultivating curiosity, openness and experimentation, artists can create fertile conditions for serendipity to flourish.

> ### Questions
>
> They say that everyone has a book in them. If you had to write a book, either fiction or non-fiction, what would it be about? What would the title be? What unexpected event or meeting in your life could form the basis for a book, a play, a song or a picture?

19
Surprising combinations

Unexpected combinations are a rich source of innovative solutions. Throughout history, some of the most transformative ideas have come from marrying elements that at first seemed unlikely or even incompatible. Whether in science, technology, art or business, strange combinations have led to unexpected solutions. When you combine two small concepts you can sometimes make a powerful third.

Combining ideas has been going on for a long time. In the ancient world one of the great discoveries was that by combining two soft metals – iron and tin – you could create a strong alloy: bronze. One of the most significant inventions of all time was the printing press. Previously all books had been laboriously copied out by hand or stamped out with woodblocks. Around 1450 in Strasbourg, France, German inventor Johannes Gutenberg combined two ideas – a coin punch and a wine press. He created a method of printing with moveable type. His invention enabled the mass production of books and the spread of knowledge and ideas throughout the Western world. In terms of revolutionizing communication, only the invention of the internet comes close.

Apple's iPhone is a masterclass in combining disparate technologies into a single impressive device. Before the iPhone, phones, cameras, computers, maps and music were mostly separate things. Steve Jobs integrated them with a touch screen and changed the world. The smartphone became a universal phenomenon and changed communication, photography and computing. It also bred an ecosystem of apps, games and developers.

You do not have to be as sophisticated as Apple to come up with clever combinations for your products. In 1972 Bernard Sadow, owner of the US Luggage company, saw a clever combination. He patented the idea of putting wheels on a suitcase. It seems obvious now but at the time it was a revolutionary concept which made moving suitcases much easier. What are the wheels that you could put on your suitcase? Like putting a bell on a clock to make an alarm clock. Or putting a camera and the internet into a phone to make a smartphone.

A striking recent example comes from Princeton University where researchers led by Professor David MacMillan discovered a novel chemical reaction through a method which they called 'accelerated serendipity'. They deliberately chose groups of chemicals that were previously thought to be unreactive with carbon and then used thousands of tests with catalysts to generate unexpected chemical combinations. They were able to combine molecules which had never before been known to interact. This discovery, rooted in deliberate exploration of unlikely pairings, offers chemists a powerful new tool for building complex molecules with potentially many uses.[23]

Food gives many examples of the power of weird combinations. Who would have thought that strawberries taste good with pepper, or bacon with chocolate, or peanut butter with pickle? These are all popular combinations. Culinary innovation thrives on unexpected pairings. Fusion cuisine blends ingredients and techniques from different countries and traditions. An example is Japanese chef and restaurateur Nobu Matsuhisa's Japanese-Peruvian cuisine. By combining the delicate flavours of Japanese sushi with the bold spices of Peruvian cooking, Matsuhisa created a unique dining experience that has delighted food lovers.

Gamification is a powerful feature to add to service offerings. Education companies like Duolingo have found that adding gaming and scoring elements to their offerings has increased their appeal. Swedish bank Ikano ran a three-week marketing campaign in 2014 with a game called 'Flappy Saver', where players controlled a flying piggy bank, avoiding crashing into stores to protect their savings. This unexpected approach made saving money engaging and fun, generating millions of plays.

Nearly every new idea is a synthesis of other ideas. So a great way to generate ideas is to force combinational possibilities. How can you do it? Get your team together and brainstorm how you could mix your products with those from wildly different sources. Take it to the extreme. How could you combine your key concept with random products, services, places, personalities, etc.? The more bizarre the combination, the more original the ideas that are triggered.

Unexpected collaborations

As well as combining odd things, we can combine odd people or organizations. Music gives many genre-bending examples. The Irish rock band U2 performed with classical tenor Pavarotti. David Bowie sang with Bing Crosby. Run-D.M.C. and Aerosmith's 'Walk This Way' fused hip-hop and rock in the 1980s. This unexpected pairing not only revitalized Aerosmith's career but also helped bring hip-hop into the mainstream.

In business, unexpected collaborations often lead to groundbreaking innovations and surprising success stories. LEGO partnered with NASA to create space-themed LEGO sets, inspiring young minds to explore science and engineering.[24] Spotify collaborated with Starbucks to allow Starbucks customers to influence in-store playlists, blending music and coffee culture. Adidas teamed up with an environmental organization, Parley for the Oceans, to produce shoes made from recycled ocean plastic. Similarly, KFC (Kentucky Fried Chicken) worked with Crocs to produce the bizarre idea of fried chicken-themed Crocs. Mercedes partnered with fashion watch maker Swatch to design its revolutionary smart car. Luxury fashion house Dolce & Gabbana collaborated with the appliance brand Smeg to create artistic kitchenware.

How can you choose who to team up with? Ideally, the partnership should be able to offer something unique that neither partner could achieve alone. Find someone who has strengths different from yours. This might be market reach, design, technology or customer experience.

Collaborating on innovative projects comes with risks. The two organizations have different processes, cultures and styles. On this joint project they need to align with a common goal and a shared vision. Clear roles and responsibilities need to be agreed early. Top-level agreement and support is needed on both sides. The prize is to bring a brilliant innovation to market.

Summary

The examples above illustrate a powerful truth: innovation often occurs with the combination of the unexpected. Look for something to add to your product to increase its appeal, like wheels on a suitcase. Look for someone who can partner with you to take you to places you have never been.

When we dare to combine strange elements, whether molecules, materials, organizations or ideas, we open the door to discoveries that conventional thinking might overlook.

Questions

Try these exercises on your own or with a team. Choose a product or service and then brainstorm many different, even absurd, things that you could combine with it. Then make a list of the types of organizations you could team up with. Name names. Take the best ideas to the next stage with a small test.

20
Unexpected failures

So far we have discussed many unexpected successes, discoveries and inventions. Let us now turn our attention to unexpected failures and disasters. What can we learn from them? We will ignore natural disasters and focus on those caused at least to some extent by human error. We will try to extract some common themes among the causes of the failures and what could have prevented them.

The Titanic, 1912

When RMS Titanic was launched it was the largest and most luxurious ship afloat. It had advanced safety features, such as watertight compartments and remotely activated watertight doors, which led to the ship's reputation as 'unsinkable'. Yet it sank on 15 April 1912 on its maiden voyage from Southampton to New York, after striking an iceberg. It was carrying some of the wealthiest people in the world, as well as hundreds of emigrants from Europe seeking a new life in the United States and Canada. Of the estimated 2,224 passengers and crew aboard, approximately 1,500 died, making the incident one of the deadliest peacetime sinkings of a single ship.

The Titanic disaster resulted from a combination of overconfidence, inadequate safety measures and poor decision-making. The 'unsinkable' ship carried insufficient lifeboats for all passengers, prioritizing deck space over safety. Captain Edward Smith maintained dangerous speed despite ice warnings, while nearby ships had turned off radios for the night. The ship's design, while advanced, couldn't withstand the massive hull breach from the iceberg impact. The news of the disaster shocked the world. The inquest showed that pride, false assumptions and overconfidence had outweighed safety concerns. The disaster led to better communication protocols and safety systems and ensured that future ships had sufficient lifeboats for all on board.

The Maginot Line, 1940

In the 1920s and 1930s British and French military leaders assumed that any new war with Germany would be fought in the same way as the World War I. France built the heavily fortified Maginot Line, named after the French Minister of War, André Maginot, along the entire border between France and Germany to prevent German invasion. But when Hitler's armies attacked in 1940, they used some lateral thinking. They simply went around the defences, through Belgium and the Ardennes Forest. French military thinking was trapped in World War I defensive strategies. However, the Germans used fast-moving blitzkrieg tactics with tanks, aircraft and paratroops completely bypassing static fortifications. France fell in just six weeks despite having superior numbers and defensive positions.

Generals often prepare for the last war rather than the next one. Military and business strategy must adapt to new technologies and tactics – old thinking can become obsolete overnight and defences can be bypassed with clever tactics.

Chernobyl, 1986

During a safety test at Ukraine's Chernobyl Nuclear Power Plant on 28 April 1986, operators disabled critical safety systems and made a series of mistakes in their procedures. When they attempted an emergency shutdown, a massive power surge caused explosions and a meltdown in a reactor. There followed a massive release of radioactive material across Europe.

The disaster stemmed from flawed reactor design, inadequate safety protocols and poor communication between personnel shifts. The accident shone a spotlight on the poor state of industrial safety, as well as on secrecy and the cover-up culture in the Soviet Union. It forced the Soviet government to become less secretive. The revelation of the cover-up of the Chernobyl disaster was a catalyst for glasnost, which paved the way for reforms leading to the collapse of the Soviet Union.[25]

Segway personal transportation, 2001–2020

American engineer Dean Kamen's Segway was hyped as a revolution in transport that was expected to transform cities. Segway is a two-wheeled, self-balancing, battery-powered electric vehicle. It was launched in 2001 in a blizzard of publicity. Yet despite $100 million in investment and predictions of selling millions of Segways annually, it never gained mainstream adoption.

Expectations were too high. The Segway was described as the future of transport. As an innovation it was said to be on a par with the PC or the internet. Inevitably it could not live up to this level of hype. PR exposure is generally useful, but this time it was overdone. The $5,000 price tag, safety concerns, regulatory restrictions, social stigma and limited practical applications all hindered success. Cities banned them from pavements and users looked awkward riding them. Production ended in 2020 after only 140,000 units had been sold over 19 years.

The failure teaches us that revolutionary technology needs a practical use. Most successful innovations involve some degree of iteration, experimentation, openness and collaboration. They need an eco-system to support them. They target users who need the benefits they offer. A radical invention with ample backing still needs to gain market acceptance. It is an uphill path and that path proved too steep for the Segway.

Friendster social network, 2002–2011

Friendster pioneered social networking before MySpace and Facebook and looked set for market domination, but the company failed because of technical problems and the inability to scale. As membership grew, reaching 115 million users at its peak, the site became painfully slow, taking minutes to load pages. Users abandoned the platform for faster alternatives like MySpace. Friendster also restricted user customization and failed to innovate quickly enough. Despite being first to market, it could not maintain its advantage. The company pivoted to gaming but eventually shut down.

Friendster's failure demonstrates that first-mover advantage does not guarantee success. Fast-growing internet companies must scale their infrastructure rapidly. The user experience is everything.

Amazon Fire phone, 2014–2015

Amazon launched the Fire Phone in 2014 with unique features like 3D interface, one-handed navigation and tight integration with Amazon services. People were curious and expectations were high. But in the end, it didn't quite land. The phone felt more like a gimmick than a game-changer. It had a weak selection of apps thanks to its customized Android system and was only available on AT&T. The fancy 3D effects also chewed through battery life without offering much real value. After a year, Amazon pulled the plug and took a $170 million loss.

The whole episode proved that even giants like Amazon can stumble. Cool features alone aren't enough; new tech needs real value for users and support from app makers and mobile carriers. Jeff Bezos later called it a 'bold bet that didn't work'.

Google Glass, 2014

Google launched Google Glass as a wearable device with built-in camera in 2013. It featured a heads-up display and voice control for hands-free tasks. It sparked intrigue but quickly ran into trouble. It cost $1,500 and faced an immediate backlash over privacy concerns, social awkwardness and limited functionality. Users were mockingly called 'Glassholes' and many establishments banned the devices. The technology wasn't ready for mass adoption, battery life was poor and the user interface was clunky. Google withdrew the consumer version in 2015.

The failure taught valuable lessons about introducing disruptive technologies gradually, addressing privacy concerns proactively and ensuring social acceptance alongside technical functionality. It also showed the importance of timing in bringing revolutionary products to market.

Summary

Although these failures are drawn from different fields, we can spot some common themes. Overconfidence and untested assumptions are major contributors to disaster. Leaders need to envisage different scenarios to the ones they are confident about. They need to ask, 'What could possibly go wrong?' Risk assessment and robust safety provision are essential. When it comes to new products, we see that even mighty companies with strong track records of innovation can get it wrong. Failure is part of business. Rapid learning and adaptation are key.

> ### Questions
>
> Consider one or two failures that you have experienced during your career. What were the causes and consequences? How much do you attribute to bad luck and how much to bad decisions? Could better planning and preparation have prevented the flops? What could you have done differently with the benefit of hindsight?

21
Serendipitous collaborations

The invention of the ice-cream cone was an accident born of serendipitous collaboration at the 1904 St Louis World's Fair in Missouri. When an ice-cream vendor ran out of dishes, he turned to a neighbouring vendor, Ernest Hamwi, who was selling waffles, for help. Hamwi quickly rolled his warm waffles into cone shapes, allowing the vendor to fill them with scoops of ice cream. The improvised solution was an instant success, pleasing customers with its novelty and convenience. This spontaneous partnership between two strangers sparked a revolutionary new way to enjoy ice cream, leading to the widespread popularity of the ice-cream cone. Their chance encounter is a prime example of how necessity and creativity can collide to create an unexpected solution.

We often picture innovation as a stroke of genius, a brilliant idea arriving in a flash of inspiration. But in reality, many of the world's cleverest inventions and breakthroughs owe their existence to something much less glamorous: a serendipitous connection with someone outside our usual circles. This means that having a diverse social network isn't just a nice-to-have, it's an engine for creativity, clever ideas and the kind of unexpected breakthroughs that can change everything.

Sociologist Mark Granovetter famously coined the term 'the strength of weak ties' to explain why it's often our more casual contacts, not our close friends, who bring us new ideas, opportunities and information. That's because they move in different circles and see different things. In short, the more diverse your network, the more likely you are to bump into fresh insights that others might miss.

So how do social networks feed innovation? It all comes down to exposure. If you only hang out with people who think like you, work like you and go to the same golf club, you are swimming in a small pond. But when you branch out and talk to people from different backgrounds, industries or cultures, your ideas are challenged and you get nudged out of your usual tracks.

Social platforms, whether it's LinkedIn, X, Instagram, Tik Tok or even your company's internal chat, can act as serendipity machines. They are a place where creative collisions can happen and where someone's casual comment might trigger your next big idea. On GitHub, for instance, developers regularly share half-finished projects, problems or puzzling code, only to find a clever idea proffered by someone thousands of miles away. It is not always intentional or deliberate. But that is the point.

InnoCentive is an open innovation platform that connects organizations with a global network of problem solvers. Companies, non-profits and government agencies post 'challenges', complex scientific, technical or business problems, on the platform. Individuals or teams from diverse disciplines submit solutions, competing for monetary rewards. What sets InnoCentive apart is its emphasis on cross-disciplinary innovation. For example, a pharmaceutical company might post a biochemical problem and receive winning ideas from a physicist or engineer. One notable case involved a NASA challenge to predict solar particle storms. A retired radio engineer, not a space scientist, provided the best solution. This crowdsourced model exploits the creativity of experts and non-experts alike, often yielding breakthrough ideas from unexpected fields. InnoCentive exemplifies how open access to challenges drives innovation across boundaries.

When individuals connect across boundaries, whether professional, cultural or social, they are exposed to novel information and alternative approaches. This exposure can lead to 'creative abrasion', a process in which ideas are tested, refined and improved through constructive debate. Moreover, diverse networks often bridge 'structural holes' – gaps between groups that otherwise wouldn't interact. Those who bridge these gaps often become 'brokers' of new ideas, introducing concepts from one domain into another where they can be recombined in innovative ways.

Examples

History is full of examples in which diverse or unexpected connections led to major breakthroughs.

John Lennon and Paul McCartney met at a church fete in Liverpool. Their musical partnership, later joined by George Harrison and Ringo Starr, blended different influences and backgrounds, revolutionizing popular music. Lennon and McCartney did not always get along. They clashed on many occasions, but they always supported each other's musical ideas.

The famous partnership that founded Apple began when mutual friend Bill Fernandez introduced Steve Jobs to Steve Wozniak. Jobs, with his vision for design and business, and Wozniak, with his technical genius, complemented each other perfectly. Their different backgrounds and skills were crucial to Apple's early success. Incidentally, Steve Jobs credited a college calligraphy class – taken on a whim after he dropped out of college – with inspiring the beautiful typography on Apple's first computers. If he'd stuck purely to engineering classes, that design elegance may never have been realized.

The founders of Google, Larry Page and Sergey Brin, met by chance at Stanford University. Page was visiting the campus and Brin was assigned to show visitors around. Despite initial disagreements, they shared an interest in data mining on the internet. Their different perspectives led to the creation of the world's most powerful search engine.

James Watson and Francis Crick met at the Cavendish Laboratory at Cambridge University in 1951. Watson, an American biologist, arrived at the laboratory after his PhD supervisor arranged for him to take up a position there. About three weeks after his arrival, Watson discovered he was sharing space in the biochemistry room with

Crick, a British physicist who had shifted to biology. Their first meeting was described as an 'instantaneous meeting of minds', with both quickly realizing their shared interest in uncovering the structure of DNA. Within minutes, they began speculating about what the structure could be, marking the beginning of their famous collaboration that led to the discovery of the double helix.

These stories all share a common thread: breakthroughs that happened not through solo genius but through unlikely connections.

Fostering serendipitous connections

The good news is that you do not have to sit around waiting for happy accidental meetings to happen. You can prepare for good fortune by being intentional about how you connect, share and collaborate.

Start by being more curious about people inside and outside your field. Chat with employees in other departments. When Nokia was a major telecom player, it had a policy of encouraging staff to take lunch in the company cafeteria and to sit with people they did not know. People learned about what has happening elsewhere in the company and many useful ideas and projects resulted.

Involve people from other sectors in your challenges and discussions. If you are working in engineering design, ask a friend in the fashion business about how they handle design problems. It is surprising how often methods, patterns and ideas translate across domains.

Share your challenges and rough ideas. A blog post about a problem or even a half-formed product idea might strike gold when someone offers an unexpected perspective. Be visible. Whether it's posting updates on your work or commenting on someone else's, stay active in diverse communities. It puts you in the path of potential ideas.

Organizations can intentionally cultivate diverse networks. Attending interdisciplinary conferences, participating in community groups or working in cross-functional teams can all increase the likelihood of serendipitous encounters. Digital social platforms and collaborative tools also make it easier to connect with people outside one's immediate circle.

Companies should encourage cross-functional teamwork. Don't keep departments in silos. Bring sales, design, engineering and customer support into the same room with a constructive facilitator and magic can happen. As mentioned before, psychological safety is crucial. We need to create safe spaces for sharing. Whether it's digital forums or casual meet-ups, people need to feel comfortable tossing out crazy ideas.

It is also worthwhile to reward exploration. Give employees space and permission to explore outside their core roles. The next big idea might come from the edge, not the centre, from the outside, not the inside.

Summary

The magic of innovation often happens from the collaboration of diverse minds. By seeking out and nurturing varied social connections, we open ourselves to new possibilities, challenge our assumptions and set the stage for transformative ideas. The stories of Jobs and Wozniak, Page and Brin, and countless others remind us that sometimes all it takes is a chance meeting and a willingness to embrace difference to change the world.

> **Questions**
>
> Take a moment to list 10 ideas for how you could seek out unfamiliar conversations and connections. Who has the skills that you lack? Who is the Pavarotti for your U2? How can you reach out to new partners in ideas both within and outside your current networks?

22
Put your product to another use

Sometimes a minor innovation in one field can become an unexpected major innovation in another. John Sipe worked in an abattoir in the US in the 1920s. Like other workers there he found that he kept slipping on the wet and bloody floors. His shoes were too slippery, so he took his knife and cut thin slits across the rubber soles. He found that the shoes now gave a much better grip. In 1923 he took out a patent on the process and called it *siping*, with the slits called sipes. He thought it could improve the grips of car tyres and he was right, but unfortunately for him siping was not adopted by the motor industry until the 1950s when superior tread compounds were developed that could stand up to the process.

On roads covered with snow, ice or water, sipes in tyres significantly improve traction. A 1978 study by the US National Safety Council found that on ice, siping improved stopping distances by 22 per cent and rolling traction by 28 per cent. The car tyre industry, and Formula One in particular, developed siping and nowadays leading shoe manufacturers borrow ideas from racing car tyres to make their shoe soles grip better – so the idea has come full circle. Incidentally, the reason the sipes work is not because they carry water away but because they make the sole much more flexible and allow a bigger area of contact and grip.

The same type of problem can exist in widely different fields – just like shoes and tyres. Look for someone who has a problem similar to yours but in a different domain. The key lies in someone recognizing that an effect in one sphere could offer a major benefit in another context entirely. How can you spot these cross-pollination opportunities? It requires both a systematic approach and deliberate practice.

A good way to approach this issue is by reframing your problem by function, not form. Instead of saying 'I need stronger tyres', say 'I need something that improves grip in wet conditions'. This functional thinking opens you to solutions from other fields, such as biology where you might think of the feet of a gecko. Or you might ponder ideas from physics like magnetic fields. Or even footwear. Try to describe your challenges in terms of the fundamental problem that needs to be solved rather than in some variant of a current approach. Describe the outcome in broad terms rather than in the tools or forms that are normal. Define what needs to happen.

Examples

Willis Carrier, an American engineer born in 1876, changed the world in a way he never expected. In 1902 he was asked to solve a humidity problem at Sackett & Wilhelms, a Brooklyn printing company. Changes in humidity caused paper to expand and contract, ruining colours during printing. Carrier's breakthrough came after a moment of inspiration while standing on a foggy Pittsburgh train platform. He realized he could control humidity by passing air through water to remove moisture. He went back to the drawing board and built a machine that could control both temperature and humidity, something nobody had done before. His invention worked so well that it not only saved the printing business but also paved the way for cool, comfortable homes, offices and theatres everywhere. Carrier patented his air-conditioning system in 1906 and what started as a fix for printers ended up changing how people live and work all over the world.

For your existing products and services, ask, 'To what other use could this be put?' Is there a bigger market for your solution in a different field? To find interesting ideas from other areas, build diverse input streams. Deliberately consume content outside your expertise. If you're in software, read materials science journals. If you're in marketing, explore neuroscience research. Set aside time weekly to explore completely unrelated fields. The goal isn't deep knowledge but broad pattern recognition.

Superglue, or cyanoacrylate, was accidentally discovered in 1942 by Harry Coover while developing clear plastic for gun sights during World War II. The compound was initially dismissed because it stuck to everything, making it impractical for manufacturing. Years later, Coover revisited the adhesive and realized its potential as a powerful bonding agent. Marketed as Super Glue, it became a household staple.

It found an unexpected application in medicine. During the Vietnam War, field medics began using Super Glue to quickly seal wounds and reduce bleeding. It was not suitable for deep cuts, but it proved highly effective for temporary closure of surface injuries, especially in combat zones. This led to the development of medical-grade variants, which are now used in hospitals for closing incisions and minor cuts. This discovery went on a journey from failed military material to household adhesive to medical lifesaver. It shows how unexpected discoveries can find new purpose in entirely different fields.

Another approach is to study similar systems. When facing a problem, ask, 'What else works this way?' or 'What has similar constraints?' Traffic-flow problems are analogous to crowd control. Marketing is sometimes likened to warfare. Product design might borrow from architecture. Collect interesting ideas, mechanisms, principles and solutions you encounter anywhere. Tag them by function rather than field. When you hit a problem, search these tags rather than your immediate domain knowledge.

There are many compelling examples of minor innovations that became transformative in different fields. QR codes started in the automotive sector but were much more influential when they moved to finance. QR codes were developed by Toyota subsidiary Denso Wave in 1994 for tracking car parts in manufacturing. This minor inventory tool became the backbone of mobile payment systems across Asia and contact-free transactions worldwide, and especially accelerated by the pandemic.

GPS was developed to aid military operations but went on to transform ridesharing. The Global Positioning System was developed for military navigation and missile guidance. This defence technology became the foundation for entirely new companies like Uber and Lyft, for industries such as food delivery and for location-based social media.

Another way of spotting opportunities is to join communities outside your field. Attend conferences, join online forums or participate in events where different disciplines intersect. These boundary spaces are where cross-pollination naturally occurs because people are already thinking beyond their primary domains.

One of my favourite stories concerns the Atlanta pharmacist John Pemberton. In 1886 he was searching for a non-addictive alternative to morphine, on which he had become dependent after a Civil War injury. He concocted a syrup using coca leaf extract and kola nuts. It was called 'Pemberton's French Wine Coca' and was marketed as a medicinal tonic and cure for headaches and fatigue. When alcohol prohibition was introduced, Pemberton reformulated the drink without wine. Then, in a lucky break, his assistant accidentally mixed the syrup with carbonated water instead of plain water. The result was surprisingly delicious and Coca-Cola was born. In 1888 Pemberton sold the recipe to Asa Griggs Candler for $239 (equivalent to about $8000 in today's money). Candler founded the Coca-Cola Company in 1892 and developed it as a major global success. What began as a failed medicinal experiment turned into one of the most iconic and profitable soft drinks in history.

Summary

Have you ever used a knife as a screwdriver or a shoe as a hammer? If so, you repurposed a product for an application that the producer did not foresee. You put the product to another use. This idea can be a fruitful source of innovations for your product or service if only you can think laterally.

De Beers is a diamond mining company founded in South Africa in 1888. It specialized in industrial diamonds, which were used as drill bits because diamonds are the hardest material found in nature. However, the company mined more diamonds than it needed for the drill business. In a brilliant and unexpected piece of marketing, the company repurposed diamonds as symbols of love and devotion. De Beers created the concept of the diamond engagement ring, with the slogan 'A diamond is forever'. It was voted the best advertising slogan of the 20th century.

Time and again we see that ideas can have a massive impact when they move from one field or application type to another. We need to keep exploring other disciplines, fields and geographies to spot ideas that we can adapt for our use and ways to repurpose our products elsewhere. The key is making this exploration systematic rather than hoping for lucky accidents.

> **Questions**
>
> Consider each of your products or services. Now brainstorm with your team what other use each could be put to. What are the core properties of the product or service? Who might need those properties in an entirely different field? Can you sell your surplus drill bits as engagement rings?

23
Trust your intuition

Business executives and MBA students are trained to use rigorous analysis, research and market studies in order to be more effective in making business decisions. But many successful entrepreneurs, innovators and business leaders eschewed these approaches and trusted their gut instinct instead.

Steve Jobs famously rejected focus groups and market research, believing that customers often don't know what they want until they see it. He trusted his intuition to guide product design, insisting on simplicity, elegance and emotional connection. Jobs once said, 'Intuition is more powerful than intellect' and credited his time studying Zen Buddhism with sharpening that instinct. His gut led Apple to create revolutionary products like the iPod, iPhone and iPad – devices that redefined entire industries. Jobs believed in following his inner compass, even when others doubted him. His ability to sense what would delight users, rather than relying on data, made him one of the most visionary leaders in tech history.

Richard Branson built the Virgin empire by trusting his instincts over plans and spreadsheets. He often made bold decisions based on gut feeling, from launching Virgin Records to challenging airline giants with Virgin Atlantic. Branson believes intuition is essential in business, especially when data can't capture human emotion or creativity. He said, 'I rely far more on gut instinct than researching huge amounts of statistics.' His approach emphasizes agility, risk-taking and style – qualities that helped Virgin stand out in crowded markets. Whether starting Virgin Galactic or entering finance with Virgin Money, Branson's intuitive leadership style has driven innovation and unexpected disruption across industries.

Intuition is not a recent concept – it has intrigued thinkers for centuries. Psychologist Carl Jung viewed intuition as one of the key ways in which our unconscious mind communicates with us, allowing quick judgements without deliberate reasoning. Today, neuroscience supports this concept by revealing that much of our brain's decision-making occurs beneath conscious awareness. Our brain detects subtle patterns and emotional cues faster than logic can catch up. This subconscious processing enables what we call 'gut feelings' – rapid, experience-based insights that guide our choices effectively, especially in complex or uncertain situations.

Trusting your intuition isn't about being random or haphazard, it's about recognizing your brain's ability to make snap judgements based on patterns, experience and subtle cues you've absorbed over time. Here are some ways to develop that ability:

- Pay attention to gut reactions. Intuition often speaks in whispers. You have a sense of excitement, ease or discomfort. Tune in to how situations or decisions make you feel, before logic takes over. Ask: 'What is my initial instinct here?'

- I believe in logic and analysis. I am a keen chess player and try to analyse the likely consequences of any move before I make it. This involves carefully studying all the possible responses and calculating a series of moves in each case. All the strong players do this, but many players, including grandmasters, will admit that sometimes, especially when they are under time pressure, they will play a move which just feels strong even though they cannot calculate all the possible outcomes. They trust their intuition, though in the case of grandmasters, this is based on playing thousands of games.

- Reflect on your past intuitive successes. Think back to moments when just following your instincts led to a good outcome. Reflecting on these experiences builds your self-confidence and reinforces an inner belief that your intuition has value. Of course, you should also remember the times you followed your gut and it did not work out. What was the difference and what can you learn?

Trusting intuition can work but it has to be tempered with common sense and investigation. Combine intuition with information. Don't rely on gut feelings in isolation. Research, analyse and then invite intuition into the mix. Balanced decisions come from blending logic and instinct, especially when facts are unclear or incomplete.

Recognizing intuition's limits

It's important to note that intuition can sometimes mislead us. Cognitive biases such as confirmation bias or overconfidence may colour our gut feelings. Emotional stress or fatigue can also distort intuitive signals. For example, anxiety might be mistaken for a warning, leading to unnecessary avoidance of risk. Recognizing these pitfalls means we should not accept every gut feeling blindly. Instead, use intuition as a prompt to pause, gather relevant facts and consider alternative viewpoints before deciding.

If you have a radical idea, seek advice from those you trust. Consult a diverse group to inform your perspective. Listen to all points of view, especially those that challenge assumption. Ponder the issue, but make the final decision alone. Don't always follow the majority opinion. Great leaders make tough decisions and this builds self-reliance and strengthens the voice within, especially when it differs from group opinion.

Summary

In sports, coaches often rely on intuition when there's no time for detailed analysis – trusting their 'feel' of the game to make split-second decisions. In science, notable breakthroughs sometimes arose when researchers trusted hunches that contradicted prevailing theories, leading to innovations that reshaped entire fields. Artists frequently follow intuition to create original works that defy conventions but resonate deeply.

Oprah Winfrey's rise from poverty to media mogul is a masterclass in trusting intuition. Early in her career, she sensed that emotional authenticity would resonate more deeply than scripted interviews. Ignoring conventional TV norms, she shared vulnerability, empathy and real human stories, transforming 'The Oprah Winfrey Show' into a cultural phenomenon. She famously avoided focus groups, relying instead on her gut to guide content and business decisions. This instinct led her to launch Harpo Productions, giving her creative control and ownership. This was unheard of for a talk-show host at the time. Her intuitive sense of timing and audience connection also fuelled the creation of the Oprah Winfrey Network (OWN), a platform for purpose-driven storytelling. Oprah's success wasn't built on data alone – it was her ability to feel what people needed before they knew it themselves that made her one of the most influential figures in media history.

Ultimately, developing trust in your intuition is not about being self-centred or fanciful. It is about building a quiet confidence in your abilities and judgement. It means learning to hear that inner whisper – and, more importantly, to not ignore it. Combining this inner voice with thoughtful analysis, mindfulness of potential biases and continual self-reflection will allow you to make wiser, more authentic decisions – whether in business, creativity or everyday life.

Questions

Do you make decisions on logical analysis or on intuition? Think back to some recent important decisions that you made. Is your sense of intuition strong or weak? Try trusting your intuition more – but still use common sense and analysis to check any decisions you make.

24
Play more

Russian scientist Dmitri Mendeleev (1834–1907) loved to play cards. In 1869, he wrote the names and properties of the 63 known elements on individual cards, then arranged and rearranged them like a game of Solitaire. He realized that elements with similar properties could be arranged in 'suits' ordered by their atomic weights. He saw patterns that weren't apparent when elements were simply listed. He moved the cards around, grouped similar elements together and saw gaps. He deduced that these gaps represented currently unknown elements. Mendeleev published his periodic table and boldly predicted the existence and properties of several missing elements, including gallium and germanium, which were later discovered exactly as he had foretold.

Work and play are often treated like oil and water, separate realms with different purposes. One is serious, structured and goal-driven; the other is spontaneous, joyful and open-ended. But for innovators like Mendeleev, these two worlds overlap. Sometimes integrating play into our daily work rhythms can unlock innovative ideas and surprising solutions. Play is not just for children or leisure. When we can weave it into our work environments, it becomes a catalyst for creativity, risk-taking and collaboration.

Play taps into our brain's reward system, releasing dopamine, which boosts motivation and cognitive flexibility. When we play, we're less afraid to fail, more inclined to take imaginative risks and better at connecting seemingly unrelated ideas. Neuroscientists and psychologists have long noted that play promotes divergent thinking, the type of thinking that leads to multiple solutions and wild ideas. It breaks us out of linear patterns and encourages exploration over efficiency, which is essential for solving complex or ambiguous problems. Play makes our brains more nimble. And nimble brains are better at sparking insights.

This does not mean turning our office into a playground. Small, intentional infusions of play can have profound effects. Turn brainstorm sessions into fun experiences by bringing in a skilled external facilitator who can use physical play objects like LEGO bricks, modelling clay or whiteboard doodles to inspire people to be outlandish and creative.

Look at ways to use gamification in customer marketing and in internal communications and contests. Award points for crazy ideas. Consider asking employees to create and perform a skit, poem or song about, say, competitors. Ask employees to pitch an idea from a rival company's perspective or imagine how a superhero might tackle the problem. These thought experiments shake up assumptions. Allow people to pursue playful side projects and innovative ideas.

American scientist Richard Feynman's playful approach to physics was central to his revolutionary discoveries. After winning the Nobel Prize, he felt burned out and decided to pursue physics purely for fun. This shift proved transformative when he began studying the wobbling motion of a spinning plate in Cornell University's cafeteria. What started as idle curiosity about the plate's wobble led him to derive the underlying equations of motion.

This playful investigation sparked insights that eventually contributed to his groundbreaking work on quantum electrodynamics. Feynman realized that the ratio between the plate's wobble and its spin was exactly 2:1, which connected to deeper principles of rotational motion and angular momentum.

His childlike wonder extended to other breakthroughs. He developed his famous Feynman diagrams by visualizing particle interactions as simple drawings, making complex quantum mechanics accessible. He approached safe-cracking, bongo playing and even biology with the same experimental playfulness. Feynman believed that maintaining curiosity and joy in discovery was essential to scientific creativity, famously saying he would only work on things that seemed interesting and fun.

Play is unpredictable by nature. It disrupts routine thinking and invites the 'what if?' question that is often the first spark of innovation. When teams play together, hierarchies soften, collaboration improves and psychological safety increases. In these moments, people feel more comfortable speaking up, asking absurd questions or suggesting unconventional ideas. Unexpected solutions often come from unexpected angles, and play creates space for exactly that.

IDEO, the world-renowned design firm, has offices that are full of toys, musical instruments and spaces that invite imaginative tinkering. The company attributes much of its creative problem-solving success to its culture of playful experimentation.

Play can be individual or social. Children love to play in small groups. At work, when colleagues share laughter or get competitive in a quiz or game, they build rapport and trust. That connection enhances team resilience and openness. This can make teams more adaptable and innovative under pressure.

Play isn't just for kids – it's a mindset that invites wonder, risk and discovery. Les Paul's revolutionary guitar innovations emerged from his relentless playing around. In the 1940s, he wasn't satisfied with the sound of hollow-body electric guitars. He began experimenting with different designs in his home workshop. His breakthrough came when he attached guitar strings and pickups to a solid piece of pine wood, creating 'The Log' – essentially the first solid-body electric guitar.

Paul's playful approach extended to recording techniques. He built his own multi-track recording equipment, overdubbing multiple guitar parts by bouncing between tape recorders. This experimentation led to his signature 'sound-on-sound' recordings with layered harmonies that seemed impossible with existing technology.

Paul's willingness to take apart, rebuild and reimagine both guitars and recording equipment transformed popular music. His playful curiosity about 'what if I try this?'

resulted in instruments and techniques that became industry standards.

A recommended game

A game which I use in brainstorm workshops is Rory's Story Cubes. It consists of nine cubes, each with six different images, giving a total of 54 little pictures. When playing the game at home, children or families roll all nine dice and then have to construct a story using all the images in any way they can. It is a surprisingly engaging game and fascinates children.

The same method can be used in a serious brainstorm environment. I recommend that you roll one or two of the dice at random and then use those images as starting points for fresh ideas. As in the random word method, you should list some associations of each image first. In my brainstorm workshops, when we run out of ideas we highlight the most promising and then roll two different cubes in order to start the process again. The process is fun and because we are using a child's game, people are more relaxed and more creative.

Summary

Of course, not every work challenge is suited to games. And people may be reluctant to join in initially. Play must be inclusive, voluntary and non-threatening. Tailor it to team dynamics and create an environment where play feels like a natural and enjoyable part of the creative agenda and not a gimmick or distraction. Leadership plays a crucial role here. When leaders model curiosity, humility and playfulness, they give others permission to do the same. It shifts the culture from performance to exploration.

Play at work isn't about being silly for the sake of it. It is about unlocking the freedom of thought that fuels ingenuity. Instead of constantly pursuing productivity, make room for joy and curiosity. It can feel counterintuitive, but the change in perspective can inspire people to be much more creative.

> ### Questions
>
> Why not play more? Introduce a little time and space at work to play games. Adopt a playful approach to your products, markets and competitors. A playful mindset will lead to unexpected ideas and suggestions.

25
Welcome the random

If you want more of the unexpected then introduce more of the random. In our carefully planned, routine-driven world, we've become immersed in predictability. This creates comfort and efficiency, but it builds invisible walls around our potential. Introducing more random influences into your life is not just about breaking routine, it is about unlocking creativity, resilience and growth that only come from welcoming uncertainty.

Random influences fundamentally rewire how our brains process information. When we encounter unexpected stimuli, our neural pathways are forced to form new connections, a process called neuroplasticity. This biological flexibility is what allows us to adapt, learn and innovate throughout our lives. Research in cognitive psychology shows that exposure to diverse, unpredictable experiences enhances creative problem-solving abilities and increases cognitive flexibility.

We have already seen how many breakthrough innovations emerged from accidental discoveries or random events. Another celebrated example concerns the American engineer and radio enthusiast Wilson Greatbatch. He was working on a device to record heart sounds when he accidentally installed the wrong resistor. The circuit emitted an electrical pulse that mimicked the human heart's rhythm. Greatbatch saw the potential in this accidental discovery and used it to invent the implantable pacemaker.

Such examples are not planned outcomes but rather the fruits of minds open to random influences and unexpected possibilities.

Break the echo chamber

Perhaps the most profound benefit of embracing randomness is its ability to shatter echo chambers. When we consistently expose ourselves to similar ideas, people and experiences, our worldview gradually narrows. Random influences act as intellectual disruption, challenging assumptions and revealing blind spots we didn't know existed.

This expansion of perspective leads to a more interesting life, but it also makes us better decision-makers. Studies show that diverse thinking leads to more innovative solutions and helps us avoid the cognitive biases that plague our thinking. It challenges the scourge of groupthink. When you randomly engage with different cultures, ideologies or disciplines, in a way you are upgrading your mental operating system.

Handling the random can help build adaptability and resilience. By regularly exposing yourself to minor unpredictabilities, you build the mental muscle needed to handle major disruptions. Random influences serve as low-stakes training for adaptability, teaching you to find opportunities within chaos and remain composed when plans fall apart.

This resilience extends beyond crisis management. People comfortable with randomness tend to be more optimistic about change, viewing unexpected events as potential adventures rather than threats. They develop what psychologists call 'uncertainty tolerance' – the ability to remain functional and even thrive when outcomes are unclear.

Practical ways to increase randomness

Here are some tactics for bringing more unpredictability into your life.

- Change your routine. Routines give us a sense of stability, but they can also limit our exposure to new experiences. Deliberately alter your daily routine. Change your morning ritual, take a different route to work. Try a random time shift. Vary when you do routine activities. Have breakfast for dinner, take walks at unusual hours or work on creative projects at times when you'd normally be doing something else. Different times of day bring different energy levels and perspectives to familiar activities. Every day do something you have never done before. These small changes can lead to new insights and ideas.

- Learn something new. Make a truly random selection of a new subject to study. For example, use the random Wikipedia article feature. Go to the library non-fiction section and take some of the first books that come to hand. Spend at least an hour diving deep into something completely outside your expertise. This practice consistently introduces new frameworks for thinking about problems.

- Deliberately seek conversations with people outside your usual circles. Attend meetings for interests you're only mildly curious about, strike up conversations with strangers in appropriate settings or join online communities discussing topics you know little about. These interactions often lead to unexpected insights and opportunities.

- Diversify the media you consume. Read publications from different political perspectives, explore genres you typically avoid or let others choose your entertainment. This isn't about consuming everything uncritically but about understanding how different minds process the same world.

- Try the 'Yes' experiment. For a short period, say 'yes' to reasonable invitations and opportunities that you'd normally decline due to comfort preferences. This might mean accepting dinner invitations to cuisines you've never tried, joining colleagues for activities outside your interests or participating in events that seem only tangentially relevant to your life.

- Acquire a new skill. Periodically pick up skills with no clear connection to your career or existing interests. Learn to juggle, study a language you have no practical need for or take up an instrument you've never considered. These seemingly 'useless' skills often connect in unexpected ways, creating unique combinations of abilities that set you apart.
- Seek strange recommendations. Ask random people you meet at work or socially to recommend books, films, TV shows or activities they love but that are unlike your normal fare. Their enthusiasm for something foreign to you can reveal hidden chances for new appreciations.
- Use randomness tools. Incorporate tools that introduce randomness into your thought processes. For example, use a series of random words from a dictionary in your brainstorm meetings. Ask the team in the meeting to force an association between the random and the brainstorm challenge. The brain is displaced and forced to approach the problem from an unexpected direction. Flip a coin, roll a dice or use a random word generator to make some choices. These tools can help you break free from habitual thinking patterns.

Overcoming resistance to randomness

The biggest obstacle to embracing random influences is often our own psychology. We are naturally loss-averse and prefer predictable outcomes. Start small with low-risk random choices, like trying a new coffee shop or taking a different walking route. As you build positive associations with unexpected experiences, you'll naturally become more comfortable with larger uncertainties.

Remember that randomness doesn't mean recklessness. You're not abandoning all planning and structure but rather creating intentional spaces for serendipity within your organized life. The goal is to loosen control and routine. You want enough unpredictability to spark growth without overwhelming your stability.

The compound effect of embracing uncertainty

Random influences create compound benefits over time. Each unexpected experience adds to your repertoire of knowledge, skills and perspectives. These seemingly unrelated elements often combine in surprising ways, leading to innovations, solutions and opportunities that wouldn't have emerged from purely logical planning.

Living with more randomness makes you a more interesting person to others and to yourself. You develop stories worth telling, perspectives worth sharing and a flexibility that serves you well in an increasingly unpredictable world. The person who embraces randomness doesn't just adapt to change, they become a catalyst for positive transformation in their own life and in the lives of others around them.

Summary

Introducing more randomness into your life can be a transformative experience. It can help you break free from routines, stimulate creativity and uncover unexpected ideas and solutions. Take deliberate actions to bring in more randomness. Embrace the unpredictable and allow yourself to explore new possibilities. By doing so, you may discover innovative solutions and gain a fresh perspective on life.

> **Questions**
>
> How can you introduce more random into your life? Change all your routines. Use a random object, picture or song to stimulate ideas, either on your own or with your team. If you have never tried the random word method, then give it a go.

26
Tell more stories

Storytelling is a powerful tool to convey ideas, share knowledge and inspire action. In the context of innovation, storytelling can act as a powerful catalyst to encourage creative thinking, risk-taking and experimentation.

Leaders who tell stories can share experiences, convey ideas in a relatable manner and inspire others to see the world differently. Stories have the power to evoke emotions, which can be a strong motivator for action. By creating an emotional connection, stories can inspire individuals to think creatively and take risks. Stories can also bring people together by providing a shared narrative and common goals. This sense of unity can foster collaboration and teamwork, which are essential for innovation. Hearing stories about how others have overcome challenges and achieved success can stimulate creative thinking and encourage individuals to explore new possibilities.

Types of stories to tell

To harness the power of storytelling to change corporate culture, it is important to know which types of stories to tell. Here are some examples:

- Personal stories are about individual experiences and journeys. They can be particularly powerful because they are relatable and evoke emotions. The account of how Oprah Winfrey overcame a difficult childhood to become one of the most influential women in the world is a powerful personal story that inspires and motivates. Can you turn parts of your life journey into a motivational story?
- Origin stories tell the tale of how something came to be. They can be particularly powerful in the context of innovation because they highlight the journey from idea to reality. The story of how Steve Jobs and Steve Wozniak founded Apple in a garage is a classic origin story that inspires entrepreneurs and innovators. It underscores the importance of passion, perseverance and thinking differently. You can share the origin stories of your organization, products or projects to inspire your team and remind them of the core values and vision that drive your work.
- Unexpected outcome stories tell of discoveries that arose from a mistake, a failed experiment or an unintended outcome. They demonstrate that sometimes, the 'wrong' path leads to the 'right' destination. The most celebrated example is Alexander Fleming's

accidental contamination of a petri dish leading to the discovery of penicillin. Perhaps you know of a product that flopped in its original intent but unexpectedly resonated with a different audience, opening a new market. These stories show that failure is not always final, it can be a stepping stone. They encourage people to look beyond initial results and explore anomalies.

- Failure stories focus on the setbacks and challenges encountered along the way. These stories can be incredibly powerful because they normalize failure and highlight the lessons learned from it. For example, you could talk about how James Dyson created more than 5,000 prototypes of his vacuum cleaner before achieving success. It shows the power of persistence and learning from failure. It is also persuasive to tell stories about your personal failures and what you learned from them. Or to tell about failures in your company's history and how they changed and maybe benefited the business.

- Customer stories are important because of the lessons learned. Showing the experiences and feedback of customers can offer valuable insights into the needs and desires of your target audience, driving customer-centric innovation. Airbnb's story of how the founders started by renting out air mattresses in their apartment to help pay the rent, and then listening to their early customers to improve their offering, is a great example of customer-driven innovation. Collect and share customer stories to keep your team focused on delivering value to your customers. Use these stories to identify opportunities for improvement and innovation.

- Collaboration stories highlight the power of teamwork and the importance of working together to achieve common goals. These stories can foster a sense of unity and encourage collaboration. The story of how the open-source community came together to develop Linux is a testament to the power of collaboration and collective innovation. Share stories of successful collaborations within your organization and beyond to show the importance of teamwork.

Remember to tell stories about ordinary people and not just geniuses and multi-millionaires. For example, let me tell you about Margaret Knight. She was born in 1838 in York, Maine. At the age of 12, Margaret witnessed a bad accident at a textile mill where a steel shuttle flew off and injured a worker. She was upset by this, but being an ingenious girl she set to work. She invented a safety device to prevent such incidents recurring. The accident prompted her lifelong interest in mechanical inventions. Years later, while working at a paper bag factory, she noticed how inefficient flat-bottom bags were to produce by hand. She sketched a design for a machine that would automatically fold and glue the bottoms of paper bags. When a man stole her idea and filed a patent, Knight fought back. She successfully proved that her design had come first. She showed ingenuity, fight and determination. She was one of the first women to receive a US patent.

Summary

Storytelling is a powerful tool that can inspire and drive innovation. By making abstract ideas tangible, fostering emotional connections and encouraging collaboration, stories can create the conditions for unexpected solutions to emerge. Whether through personal stories, origin stories, unexpected outcomes, failure stories, customer stories or collaboration stories, the art of storytelling can be a catalyst for innovation.

Steve Jobs said, 'The most powerful person in the world is the storyteller. The storyteller sets the vision, values and agenda of an entire generation that is to come.' Embrace the art of storytelling and let it be a catalyst for your innovation.

By intentionally weaving these narratives into the daily life of an organization or community, 'storytelling serendipity' transforms individual moments of good fortune into a collective wellspring of unexpected solutions, fostering a dynamic environment ripe for continuous innovation.

> **Questions**
>
> This book offers many examples of people who found unexpected solutions. Can you select three or four of your favourites? Research them in a little more detail and then use them with your team to illustrate the key points that you want to convey. Stories are more effective than lectures.

27
Accept productive boredom

In today's busy world, we have developed a strong aversion to boredom. The moment our minds begin to wander, we reach for our phones, check email or find some other distraction. Yet in doing so, we are systematically destroying one of the most powerful stimuli for unexpected solutions: unstructured mental downtime.

The neuroscience is clear. When we're not actively focused on a task, our brains do not simply shut down. Instead, they enter what researchers call the 'default mode network'. This is a state where different regions of the brain begin working in ways that do not happen during focused attention. This is when disparate memories, experiences and knowledge fragments start making unexpected connections. It is during these moments of apparent mental idleness that our most creative insights often emerge.

The paradox of productive procrastination

Adam Grant, an organizational psychologist, talks about the power of 'productive procrastination'. In his research, Grant found that his most original ideas came not when he rushed to complete projects but when he allowed himself to sit with problems for extended periods. He would start thinking about a research question, then deliberately delay diving into the work, letting his mind wander and explore tangential connections.

This approach led to some of his most useful insights. His research on 'giver' versus 'taker' personalities in organizations emerged during a period when he was supposed to be working on an entirely different project. By allowing his mind to procrastinate productively, he stumbled upon connections between generosity and professional success that had eluded other researchers.

The key distinction Grant discovered was between active procrastination, where you consciously delay while your mind continues to work on the problem, and passive procrastination, where you simply avoid the work altogether. Active procrastination creates the conditions for serendipity by keeping the problem alive in your subconscious while your conscious mind explores related territories.

The default mode advantage

Lin-Manuel Miranda's creation of the musical 'Hamilton' perfectly illustrates how boredom can stimulate unexpected solutions. The idea struck him on holiday while he was reading Ron Chernow's biography of Alexander Hamilton. He wasn't trying to write a musical; he was simply allowing his mind to wander while absorbing the story. The unexpected connection between Hamilton's life and modern hip-hop culture emerged precisely because Miranda's mind was in a relaxed, receptive state.

This phenomenon occurs because the default mode network excels at making remote associations, connections between seemingly unrelated concepts that our focused attention would never pursue. When we're actively concentrating on a problem, our brains tend to follow predictable, logical pathways. But when we're bored, our minds become more likely to make those unexpected leaps that lead to breakthrough insights.

Ways to find space for productive boredom

The challenge is that genuine boredom has become increasingly rare. We've filled every possible moment of downtime with activity. Yet creating space for productive boredom doesn't require dramatic lifestyle changes, it needs you to deliberately create some space.

The most successful practitioners of productive boredom don't wait for it to happen accidentally, they deliberately design it into their routines. This requires a fundamental shift in how we think about productivity and time management.

Steve Jobs was famous for his walking meetings, but equally important were his solitary walks. Research shows that walking, particularly in natural settings, activates the brain networks associated with creative insight. The rhythmic, automatic nature of walking frees up cognitive resources for making unexpected connections. I like to walk with earphones and listen to podcasts. But I get my best ideas when I leave the podcast alone and just wander.

Before smartphones, commutes were natural incubators for unexpected ideas. The combination of routine activity (driving or travelling on public transport) and mental freedom created ideal conditions for serendipitous thinking. Nowadays everyone on the train is glued to their device. Try reclaiming at least part of your commute from digital distraction to let your mind wander.

Like many people I find that I have some of my best ideas in the shower. The combination of warm water, routine physical activity and freedom from external input creates an ideal environment for default mode network activation. Extending this principle, any routine physical activity performed without external stimulation can become a creativity catalyst.

When working on writing assignments I use the Pomodoro Technique, which was designed to improve personal productivity. It was created by Francesco Cirillo in the 1980s and named after the Italian word for tomato.

It involves breaking tasks into 25-minute periods, each called a pomodoro. After each pomodoro there is a short break. Most people would plunge into emails, but I try to use these breaks to give me the opportunity to allow my mind to wander. These seemingly 'unproductive' moments often generate the insights that make your subsequent focused work far more effective.

Try dedicating one hour each week to completely unstructured time. No agenda, no goals, no devices, just mental freedom to explore wherever your thoughts lead. This isn't leisure time; it is strategic boredom designed to generate unexpected connections.

The art of marination

Srinivasa Ramanujan, the brilliant Indian mathematician, had an unusual problem-solving approach. Rather than tackling mathematical problems directly, he would write them on a slate and simply live with them for days or weeks. He would not actively work on them but would allow the problems to 'marinate' in his subconscious while he went about his daily activities. This approach led to some of the most profound mathematical insights of the 20th century.

Modern research validates Ramanujan's intuitive approach. Studies show that people who are given a problem, then become distracted with an unrelated task, often outperform those who work on the problem continuously. The distraction period allows the subconscious mind to continue processing while the conscious mind rests, often leading to more creative solutions.

Summary

Productive boredom is different from idleness or restlessness. It involves a sense of receptive alertness. You are not seeking specific stimulation, but you are open to whatever emerges. Your mind might feel like it is gently floating between different thoughts and memories, making connections you wouldn't normally notice.

The key is learning to distinguish between this fertile mental state and the anxiety-driven boredom that makes us reach for distractions. Productive boredom feels spacious and open; destructive boredom feels tight and urgent.

The benefits of embracing productive boredom compound over time. As you become more comfortable with unstructured mental time, your brain develops stronger default mode network connections. You become more skilled at recognizing when insights are emerging and less impatient in looking for immediate solutions.

Perhaps most importantly, you begin to trust the process. Instead of feeling guilty about moments of apparent mental idleness, you recognize them as essential components of your creative toolkit. This shift in perspective transforms 'wasted' time into strategic investment in unexpected solutions.

In a world that increasingly encourages speed and constant activity, the ability to be productively bored becomes a significant competitive advantage. It is not about doing less; it is about creating the mental conditions where your most unexpected and valuable ideas can emerge.

> ### Questions
>
> Make a note of three things that you can do to give yourself more unstructured time during which you can let your mind wander in a creative zone. Can you try this over the next week?

28
AI can aid the unexpected and innovation

We tend to think that creativity is for humans and not computers, but the lines are blurring. Artificial intelligence (AI) and advanced technologies can be used as tools for creativity, serendipitous discovery and innovation. Rather than viewing AI as a replacement for human imagination, I think it can be seen as a powerful creative partner. Technology, and especially AI, can help create the conditions for unexpected solutions, novel ideas and breakthrough innovations.

Generative AI tools like Microsoft Copilot, ChatGPT, Mistral, Claude and Google's MusicLM allow users to produce poems, stories, images, songs and designs by describing their requirements in plain language. These platforms function as idea partners, helping users break through creative blocks or explore new directions they might not have considered.

For example, scriptwriters in Hollywood have begun using AI to generate character types, dialogue drafts or alternative plotlines. While the final output remains a human creation, AI can provide an initial 'messy draft' or stimulate lateral thinking. Similarly, architects and designers now use generative design platforms such as Autodesk Dreamcatcher, which can suggest thousands of possible structural variations based on goals and constraints, fostering previously unimagined solutions.

In music, artist Holly Herndon uses an AI version of her own voice, dubbed 'Spawn', as a collaborative instrument. This allows her to layer machine-generated vocals with her live performance, producing original compositions that combine human and artificial creativity.

Designing for serendipity

Serendipity is difficult to engineer but AI platforms can enhance the chance of unexpected connections. For instance, Spotify's algorithm has become famous for introducing users to previously unknown music based on their listening patterns. While designed for entertainment, this principle has powerful implications for learning and innovation. Imagine an AI platform that connects a biotech researcher in India with a materials scientist in Sweden because their published data shares a subtle overlap. AI makes this type of discovery possible at scale.

LinkedIn's 'People You May Know' and GitHub's project recommendation engine provide similar functions in professional domains. These tools help users find collaborators or projects they weren't actively searching for. This can spark new ideas and partnerships. AI can be a digital matchmaker for creativity.

AI pattern recognition

AI thrives on pattern recognition. When applied to large datasets, it can uncover hidden insights that lead to innovation or solutions to long-standing problems. A well-known case involved the US retailer Target. The company used AI to identify pregnant customers based on seemingly unrelated shopping habits such as buying particular lotions and vitamins. Though controversial, this example demonstrates AI's capacity to detect patterns that human analysts might miss, opening the door to new strategies, products or interventions.

In healthcare, DeepMind's AlphaFold revolutionized biology by solving the protein-folding problem, a scientific challenge that had stumped researchers for 50 years. By training its models on vast biological data, AlphaFold accurately predicted the 3D structure of proteins. This led to new drug discoveries and disease research worldwide. These breakthroughs emerged because AI was able to analyse information at a scale and speed impossible for humans. AI can give unexpected insights with real-world impact.

Create the environment

Technology can assist innovation if it is used in a supportive ecosystem. It needs to be embedded in a culture that is open to experimentation and crazy ideas. Organizations like IDEO, Google X and MIT Media Lab thrive by creating environments where AI, design thinking and cross-disciplinary collaboration intersect. These spaces provide not just tools but mindsets: psychological safety, permission to play, tolerance for ambiguity and curiosity over certainty.

In the corporate world, tools like Miro (visual collaboration) and Notion (knowledge management) are now augmented with AI to help teams summarize discussions, extract tasks from notes or even suggest next steps in a brainstorming session. When used well, these tools don't constrain creativity, they accelerate it.

AI can lower the barriers to entry for creativity. In the past, producing music, designing a product or building a website required specialized skills and expensive tools. Today, AI-powered platforms allow anyone to experiment. Canva uses AI to generate design layouts, recommend colour palettes and adjust visual effects. RunwayML lets users generate video content using simple prompts, with no editing expertise required. Entrepreneurs can use generative tools like these to prototype business models or pitch decks.

AI risks

There are risks. AI, if poorly designed or overused, can lead to uniform thinking. Recommendation algorithms can reinforce existing preferences and prejudices. Moreover, the ease of generating ideas might encourage laziness, where you accept the first AI suggestion rather than pushing on for something more original. To avoid these pitfalls, I recommend that you apply critical thinking and use AI results as a starting point rather than a final result. Think of AI as an enabler of curiosity, a source of ideas that will stimulate your human ingenuity.

Moreover, even the apparent flaws of AI can be a source of innovation. The 'hallucinations' or unexpected and sometimes nonsensical outputs of generative AI should not always be dismissed as errors. They can be a bizarre form of input. An architect asking AI to design a building and receiving a structurally impossible but aesthetically fascinating concept could be inspired to incorporate those novel shapes into a real-world design. Weird results can push the boundaries of our creativity.

Recommendations for using AI

Individuals can use AI to brainstorm alternatives, challenge assumptions or test hypotheses. You can explore AI-generated content as a way to step outside your comfort zone. You should regularly revisit AI outputs with a critical lens, asking, 'What's surprising? Does this feel right?' You should use and combine multiple tools (text, image, data) for richer, multimodal creativity.

Organizations should create protected time and space for employees to explore AI tools beyond their daily tasks. They can use AI to facilitate cross-functional collaboration, connecting departments or individuals. Internal platforms can be used for sharing AI-generated ideas, encouraging remixing and iteration. AI should be incorporated into new product development processes, for example by using generative models during design sprints.

Summary

Creativity has always been about making new connections, from Picasso's blending of African art and cubism to Steve Jobs' fusion of technology and liberal arts. Now we have tools capable of making those connections faster, deeper and more surprising than ever before.

AI and technology do not replace human creativity. They can augment it, remove bottlenecks and open new doors. The innovative breakthroughs of the future are likely to emerge from machines and humans working in collaboration.

Questions

List the different generative AI models that you will try for maybe the first time. Think of new challenges and prompts that will give you stimulating ideas for your pressing problems. How many different generative AI tools have you tried?

29
Build a physical environment for serendipity

Is it possible to create a physical environment that encourages serendipity and unexpectedly beneficial ideas? Surprisingly, I think the answer is yes. Many companies are doing just that. We learned during the working-from-home period that the benefit of chance encounters and random conversations was lost. There is plenty of evidence that these fortuitous meetings cultivate collaborative ideas and innovations. Organizations have found that by designing physical spaces that facilitate these interactions, they can release the creative potential of their staff and foster a culture of innovation. For example, the Royal Society of Art in London redesigned its central atrium into a coffee shop modelled on the famous coffee shops of Vienna, which were meeting places for great minds and great ideas.

Serendipity is defined as beneficial results from chance events. As we have seen, it has often played a key role in creativity, innovation and discoveries. When people with different skills and backgrounds meet, they can share ideas, perspectives and knowledge that may lead to surprising ideas and innovations. Can you organize your space to facilitate these serendipitous and unplanned meetings?

Many leading companies are doing just that. The Massachusetts Institute of Technology (MIT) enhanced its reputation as a hub of innovation and collaboration with its so-called Infinite Corridor. This is a long passage that connects different parts of the campus. Along this hallway there are cafés, lounges and study spaces – all designed to encourage spontaneous connections between people, whether faculty members, students or staff.

Similarly, Pixar Animation Studios is renowned for its salubrious communal spaces. Its buildings are designed to inspire people from different departments to socialize and share ideas. The aim is to develop collaboration and a culture of creativity. The headquarters has a large central hall with a café and comfortable spaces to sit and meet. This central hub is a deliberate design choice, forcing people from different disciplines to cross paths and interact. This concept extends to the strategic placement of amenities. At Pixar, the only restaurant, the main toilets and the primary postboxes are all located in this central atrium, compelling even the most introverted employees to venture out of their offices and into the communal heart of the building.

Build a physical environment for serendipity

At a simpler level, open and flexible workspaces can help to foster serendipitous encounters. Companies can create an environment that encourages movement and chance meetings by removing physical barriers such as walls and cubicles. Open workspaces mean that people can see each other and start conversations more easily. By encouraging spontaneous collaboration, a community of ideas and creativity can be developed. For example, Google's offices are famous for their open layouts. They offer people the chance to mix and chat, with shared workspaces and communal areas such as lounges, cafés and kitchens. This design layout reinforces the company's reputation for innovation and creativity.

However, the move towards open-plan offices is not without its critics. A potential downside is the lack of privacy and the difficulty of finding quiet spaces for focused work. To counteract this, a successful design must incorporate a variety of spaces, from bustling social hubs to quiet, library-like zones, allowing employees to choose an environment that suits their immediate needs.

One design layout technique that seems to help promote serendipitous encounters is the clever placement of shared amenities such as toilets, printers, coffee machines and water coolers. By getting people to leave their usual surroundings to use these amenities, we can create natural gathering points where employees are likely to meet and chat. The offices of the renowned design and innovation company, IDEO, include mixed-use spaces that combine workstations, meeting areas and relaxation zones. This layout encourages movement, chance encounters, collaboration and creative conversations.

Another effective strategy is the creation of 'third spaces' – areas that are neither a formal workstation nor a designated meeting room. These can be comfortable alcoves with soft seating, a small library or even a games area. These spaces signal that it's acceptable to take a break from one's desk and engage in more informal, and often more creative, interactions.

Research has shown that exposure to natural elements can reduce stress and improve the feeling of well-being. Organizations can inspire and energize staff by designing workspaces that include plants, natural light and water features. A spectacular illustration is Amazon's spherical headquarters in Seattle. This building was designed to revel in verdant plants and natural light. It comprises three huge spherical domes covered in glass pentagons. The complex houses some 40,000 plants, as well as meeting spaces, lounges and retail stores. The largest dome is four stories tall. The domes were nicknamed 'Bezos's balls' by the media and have become a major tourist attraction. The building encourages employees to move around and meet each other in a visually inspiring setting. It has enhanced Amazon's reputation for flair and innovation.

Furthermore, researchers have discovered that the height of the ceiling in a meeting room can affect the outcome of the meeting. Apparently, a high ceiling encourages people to think more creatively, with big bold ideas, while a low ceiling discourages imagination and influences people to think in a constrained way. If you want a productive brainstorm meeting, meet somewhere with plenty of headroom. The tall spaces in the Amazon headquarters show this in action.

Summary

Creating a physical environment that encourages serendipitous meetings and chance encounters will promote collaborative conversations, unexpected ideas and a culture of creativity. Ideally your building should include open, flexible workspaces, high ceilings, natural light, plant life, communal areas and mixed-use spaces. This will encourage movement, mixing and opportune encounters. If we cannot afford what Amazon, Google, Pixar, MIT or IDEO have done, we can at least learn some lessons and emulate them in a small way. Making changes to the physical environment and encouraging more informal meetings will help foster collaborative ideas and breakthrough innovations.

Questions

Think about all the places you have worked. Which were constraining and which were empowering? Were there opportunities for random meetings and 'water cooler moments'? How would you feel about working in the Amazon offices described above?

Conclusion

There is a famous story of an event that took place at the Moon's Lake House restaurant in Saratoga Springs, New York, in the summer of 1853. A particularly demanding customer (who might have been the railroad and shipping magnate Cornelius Vanderbilt) repeatedly sent his order of french-fried potatoes back to the kitchen, complaining that they were too thick and not crispy enough. This annoyed the chef, George Crum. In a moment of pique, Crum decided to teach the fussy customer a lesson. He sliced the potatoes paper-thin, fried them to a brittle crisp in hot oil and, for good measure, doused them with an extra helping of salt. To Crum's astonishment, the customer, instead of being insulted, was delighted with the 'Saratoga Chips', as they came to be known. The accidental creation was an instant success and what are known as chips in the US and crisps in the UK were born.

This final example of many in this book bears all the classic hallmarks of an unexpected solution. Repeated trials and failures, annoyance, frustration and radical action led to a surprising success.

Similar unexpected successes can occur in any field at any time. The key message from this book is that although chance plays a big part, the conditions for successful serendipity can be cultivated. At a personal level we need to be curious and open-minded, ready to challenge assumptions and countenance strange notions. We need to relentlessly ask searching questions. We should deliberately step outside our comfort zone and encounter new people and experiences.

In business we need to create an atmosphere of psychological safety where people are free to voice controversial ideas without fear of criticism. We need to encourage people to experiment without fear of blame for failure. We should encourage collaboration between people working in widely different disciplines. We should use tools including AI to develop and test radical ideas.

I would recommend that you look back at the chapters and ideas that inspired you. Look at the suggested actions and the ones you chose as most appropriate for you and your organization. I urge you to put these methods into use.

These approaches will likely lead to beneficial and sometimes brilliant innovations. But I believe that there are better reasons to adopt them. At a personal level you will be a more interesting person, leading a more interesting life. At a corporate level you will create an organization that is fun to work for and can attract and retain talented people. You must agree that these are good reasons for action.

Notes

1 Daniel Kahneman (2012) *Thinking, Fast and Slow*, Penguin
2 Adam Grant (2021) *Think Again*, W H Allen
3 Christian Busch (2020) *The Serendipity Mindset*, Riverhead Books
4 Neurosciencenews.com (archived at https://perma.cc/32SN-REGH) (2024) Creativity's neural origin revealed, https://neurosciencenews.com/creativity-dmn-neuroscience-26436 (archived at https://perma.cc/B7QK-4UL4)
5 National Library of Medicine, https://pmc.ncbi.nlm.nih.gov/articles/PMC10461810 (archived at https://perma.cc/DRE9-ETP2)
6 Chengwei Liu and Mark de Rond (2019) In search of behavioral opportunities from misattributions of luck, *Academy of Management Review*
7 David Laws (2024) Fifty years of the personal computer operating system, https://computerhistory.org/blog/fifty-years-of-the-personal-computer-operating-system (archived at https://perma.cc/XU3V-4VVY)
8 Peter Westberg (2024) Microsoft's journey to becoming the world's most valuable company, https://quartr.com/insights/company-research/microsofts-journey-to-becoming-the-worlds-most-valuable-company (archived at https://perma.cc/YJK4-U3Q6)
9 Barbara Weltman (2024) Are you lucky? This matters to business success, https://bigideasforsmallbusiness.com/are-you-lucky-this-matters-to-business-success (archived at https://perma.cc/9GWF-NDVZ)

10 Richard Wiseman (2004) *The Luck Factor*, Arrow

11 Brett G Friedman (2020) How Booking.com (archived at https://perma.cc/83DB-N9T8) uses 1000s of experiments to build a culture of scientists, Medium.com (archived at https://perma.cc/4B7M-6F5P), https://brettgfriedman.medium.com/how-booking-com-uses-1000s-of-experiments-to-build-a-culture-of-scientists-b99b349c37d6 (archived at https://perma.cc/2425-LC8C)

12 Karen Walker (2024) Why building a culture of experimentation is worth the risk, *Forbes*, www.forbes.com/sites/karenwalker/2024/10/21/why-building-a-culture-of-experimentation-is-worth-the-risk (archived at https://perma.cc/U3RC-T4F4)

13 Eric Ries (2011) *The Lean Startup*, Portfolio Penguin

14 Stuart Brameld (2022) Steven Bartlett on building a culture of experimentation, https://growthmethod.com/experimentation-culture/?utm_source=chatgpt.com (archived at https://perma.cc/SH7P-9Q23)

15 Alessandro Marianantoni (2025) From test results to business decisions: The learning loop, Maccelerator, https://maccelerator.la/en/blog/startups/from-test-results-to-business-decisions-the-learning-loop (archived at https://perma.cc/Q4JS-CP3J)

16 Ed Catmull and Amy Wallace (2014) *Creativity Inc.*, Random House

17 *Daily Telegraph* (2014) Can the Japanese car factory methods that transformed a Seattle hospital work on the NHS? 3 July

18 Association for Psychological Science (2014) Observation skills may be key ingredient to creativity, www.psychologicalscience.org/news/minds-business/observation-skills-may-be-key-ingredient-to-creativity.html (archived at https://perma.cc/7LUQ-YG3Z)

19 Carol Dweck (2012) *Mindset: How you can fulfil your potential*, Robinson

20 Tim Harford (2016) *Messy: How to be creative and resilient in a tidy-minded world*, Little, Brown
21 Eric Ries (2011) *The Lean Startup*, Portfolio Penguin
22 Evelyn Fox Keller (1983) *A Feeling for the Organism: Life and work of Barbara McClintock*, W H Freeman
23 https://blogs.princeton.edu/research/2013/03/29/serendipity-pays-off-science (archived at https://perma.cc/AW54-QUN9)
24 www.imaxdigital.com/unusual-brand-collaborations-that-actually-worked (archived at https://perma.cc/85GS-XAKE)
25 NBC News (2006) Chernobyl cover-up a catalyst for glasnost, www.nbcnews.com/id/wbna12403612 (archived at https://perma.cc/W7HG-ZEAF)

Looking for another book?

Explore our award-winning books from global business experts in Skills and Careers

Scan the code to browse

www.koganpage.com/sce

More skills and career books from Kogan Page

ISBN: 9781398621008

ISBN: 9781398622944

ISBN: 9781398607064

ISBN: 9781398607941

www.koganpage.com

From 4 December 2025 the EU Responsible Person (GPSR) is:
eucomply oÜ, Pärnu mnt. 139b – 14, 11317 Tallinn, Estonia
www.eucompliancepartner.com

www.ingramcontent.com/pod-product-compliance
Lightning Source LLC
Chambersburg PA
CBHW010447010526
44118CB00021B/2527